USING FORENSIC DNA EVIDENCE AT TRIAL

A Case Study Approach

D1333659

USING FORENSIC DNA EVIDENCE AT TRIAL

A Case Study Approach

Jane Moira Taupin
Melbourne, Victoria, Australia

CRC Press
Taylor & Francis Group
Boca Raton London New York

CRC Press is an imprint of the
Taylor & Francis Group, an **informa** business

CRC Press
Taylor & Francis Group
6000 Broken Sound Parkway NW, Suite 300
Boca Raton, FL 33487-2742

© 2016 by Taylor & Francis Group, LLC
CRC Press is an imprint of Taylor & Francis Group, an Informa business

No claim to original U.S. Government works

Printed on acid-free paper
Version Date: 20160126

International Standard Book Number-13: 978-1-4822-5581-2 (Paperback)

Visit the Taylor & Francis Web site at
http://www.taylorandfrancis.com

and the CRC Press Web site at
http://www.crcpress.com

Printed and bound by CPI Group (UK) Ltd, Croydon, CR0 4YY

Contents

CHAPTER 1 — **History of DNA Profiling Evidence in
the Judicial System** 1

List of Figures

List of Tables

Preface

Purpose of This Book

This text aims to provide a knowledge base for the criminal trial attorney/lawyer/barrister utilising a trial case approach with which they are familiar. The example case studies provided highlight the strengths and limitations of DNA evidence and its practical application in court. The text is designed specifically for the criminal lawyer and written in an accessible manner for the non-scientific reader – although necessary scientific terms are employed.

It follows from *Introduction to Forensic DNA Evidence for Criminal Justice Professionals* by this author, but may be read independently. The technical aspects of forensic DNA evidence are not covered as in the first book but are referred to with the many references that should be recognised in the scientific literature by forensic scientists giving testimony. These references will be useful for the trial lawyer in examination and cross-examination of the expert witness.

A few texts have discussed a rigorous court testimony approach, based on previous cases, to analyse and deconstruct the forensic DNA evidence so that other criminal justice professionals can utilise this information in their own case. This text is not a descriptive narrative, although it necessarily includes a description of the particular alleged offence, court and any subsequent proceedings for a full picture.

All sides of the adversarial system should be confident and aware of the strengths and limitations of the DNA evidence in a case in order for the criminal justice system to operate effectively. This book aims to assist in this process so that the trial lawyer can confidently understand and convey this innovative technology. It aims to provide the trial lawyer with information to determine whether the conclusions in a forensic report are supported by the data or perhaps require further expert advice to assist in this determination. DNA profiles that require special considerations are discussed – partial, low level or mixtures – so that the trial attorney will be alerted to potential problems.

DNA offers a degree of certainty often missing in a criminal trial. It helps focus police investigations and solve cold cases decades old. Alternatively, the investigating police may be happy with a DNA result(s) and become complacent, and other avenues remain unexplored or are unsatisfactory. The lawyer for any party should be aware of biased or sloppy investigations. Even if there is overwhelming evidence of guilt, DNA profiling should still be considered, as the "Innocence Project" has repeatedly shown. If there appear to be no relevant or missing exhibits, what else can be done?

The text also discusses the nature of expertise, especially the role of subjectivity in the interpretation of forensic DNA evidence, and emphasises cognitive bias and extraneous context.

Scope

This book is designed for the lawyer or other legal professional (such as a judge or advisor) with limited scientific knowledge. However, forensic scientists and those with an interest in the application of DNA to criminal proceedings should also find it instructive. Hence, it should be thought-provoking reading for crime authors, journalists and legal commentators.

The text is mainly limited to the most common DNA methods used in criminal trials today – STR techniques used in traditional nuclear DNA typing, and the lineage markers of mitochondrial and Y-STR typing. Statistics discussed are the probabilities obtained in comparison of reference samples and crime scene samples. Novel techniques which have been recently introduced, such as familial testing and domestic animal hair, are explored. Paternity statistics are not discussed.

The book will be more applicable to the adversarial system with trial and jury encountered in countries such as England, the United States and Australia, although many of the principles can be applied to other countries without a jury such as those in Europe (with a panel of judges) or those in the Middle East and Asia (with a single judge).

Specific forensic DNA issues are illustrated with court proceedings such as trials and appeals, commissions of inquiry and government reviews. Exonerations through DNA testing will highlight the strengths and limitations of such evidence.

Acknowledgements

I thank my editor Mark Listewnik at Taylor & Francis Group for his enthusiasm and interest regarding this book.

I thank my previous editor Becky Masterman, who encouraged me to write.

I thank Dr. Angela Gallop of the United Kingdom who inspired as a laboratory director and who remains a role model in the practice of forensic science. I thank Professor Peter Gill of Norway for his continuing advice regarding some difficult DNA problems.

I also thank the many barristers and lawyers I have worked with, who have devoted considerable time and effort in understanding a topic that is often alien to legal personnel. This book is for barristers, lawyers and attorneys that are confronted with a DNA report. I hope you find it useful.

Author

Jane Moira Taupin earned her bachelor of science (honours) from the University of Melbourne, Parkville, Victoria, Australia. Upon graduating, she accepted research positions at the University of Melbourne research facilities, first in antibody production at the Howard Florey Institute and then in cancer research at the Austin Hospital. She joined the Australian Federal Police as a constable and then stage 1 detective and worked in diverse areas, including drug surveillance and government fraud. During this time, she was transferred temporarily to the only atomic energy facility in the country (Lucas Heights) which used neutron activation analysis on a number of criminal cases. She left to join the Victoria Police Forensic Services Centre as a forensic scientist, where she reported a wide variety of cases involving biological evidence in major crime. This included attendance at scenes of crime for blood pattern analysis and searching for biological fluids. She has presented biological expert evidence in courts of law and DNA profiling evidence in court since 1999. Concurrently, she earned a post-graduate diploma in criminology and then a master of arts in criminology, both from the University of Melbourne. Her master's thesis in 1994 on the impact of DNA profiling was one of the first in the field.

Jane then moved to Forensic Alliance in England, where she performed similar work in their Oxford and Manchester laboratories. When LGC Forensics took over that company, she joined as a lead scientist. In December 2009, she returned to Melbourne and was employed at MRS Limited as an international forensic auditor and lectured in Qatar and Bahrain on a variety of subjects, including DNA analysis. She is currently an independent forensic consultant and trainer.

Jane has published many articles in peer-reviewed journals on trace evidence, clothing damage and blood pattern analysis and has co-authored a text on the forensic examination of clothing. She won a Young Investigators Award from the International Association of Forensic Sciences to attend their meeting in Tokyo in 1996 for her work on clothing damage analysis. The following year, she won an Australian Government Michael Duffy travel fellowship to attend the American Academy of Forensic Sciences meeting in New York and international laboratories, including the FBI, the Forensic Science Service in England and the BKA in Germany. She was invited and participated on the inaugural committee of SWGMAT (Scientific Working Group on Materials) under the auspices of the FBI in Washington, DC, for six years. In 2009, she was awarded a 'Good Citizen Award' from Greater Manchester Police in England for her work in helping to solve a horrific rape case on an elderly woman through DNA profiling evidence.

Jane authored a text on DNA profiling in criminal cases for the legal and forensic communities in 2013. She is a forensic science consultant in Australia.

Chapter **1**

History of DNA Profiling Evidence in the Judicial System

Introduction

DNA profiling was first used in a double murder investigation in 1986 (Case 1.1). Since that date, there has been exponential growth in the use of the technique. A forensic scientist desires better tools to discriminate biological matter. A crime investigator desires the latest technology to determine 'a person of interest' or to eliminate potential suspects. The media including newspaper columns, film and television capitalizes on the fascination of the public with crime – who, what, when, where and how the crime was committed – to engage the reader and viewer.

Forensic science laboratories replaced their less discriminatory biological tests, for example ABO grouping, with DNA profiling. The first decade involved DNA testing on a sufficient quantity and quality of matter – visible blood stains or medical swabs with quantities of sperm. Improvements such as innovative copying technology dramatically increased the value of small and often degraded crime samples. Material that cannot be seen by the naked eye, such as tiny bloodstains, and exhibits that have merely been handled or 'touched' are now routinely analyzed for DNA.

The techniques for the analysis and interpretation of DNA testing have changed over the decades. Without doubt there will be further advances in the scientific process and thus further evaluation of the science, as applied, will be necessary. The forensic geneticist continually aims to improve their identification tools.

DNA profiling is used to investigate 'cold cases' in which DNA analysis was not used or where there was doubt about the correct application of a forensic technique. Persons of interest have been identified which had previously not been possible. The DNA isolated from the matter is more stable and less subject to bacterial or environmental attack than previous biological markers. Possible errors in past criminal cases have been shown. The Innocence Project in New York has used DNA profiling to investigate original convictions and has been instrumental in overturning more than 300 of these (see Innocence Project website www.innocenceproject.org for examples).

But DNA must be present on evidentiary items for this to be done – exhibits have been lost and destroyed, and material decomposed in some of these old cases. There may not be any biological evidence in the case. Furthermore, is the DNA relevant and if so, how is this relevance defined?

Historic cases may illustrate issues that are still debated. Scientific and legal acceptance of new techniques, reliability and validity of the particular process, contamination and other errors were discussed in the historic cases described in this chapter. It may be that the trial process will address an issue that has not been fully debated or reached consensus in scientific circles. It may also be that a scientific topic is not fully addressed in the legal process.

A DNA result must be considered in context. Because of the often enormous numbers statistically generated in reports, there must be a consideration of all processes, including those from the time of the collection of the sample to the final report outlining the evidential weight.

Principles of science, and interpreting scientific data, were reiterated in a 2009 U.S. study on forensic science (National Research Council, 2009). Reproducibility and validity should be considered in every forensic process. The scientific method is paramount.

It is essential to articulate the reasoning process in a forensic examination and the context associated with the evidence that is being evaluated. The chapters in this book will discuss these issues.

Introduction of the Technique

The first murders solved by DNA profiling were in England in the mid-1980s (Jobling and Gill, 2004; Wambaugh, 1989). The investigation precipitated the use of forensic DNA profiling internationally.

CASE 1.1   Exclusion of Initial Accused; Intelligence Screen; Biological Link

A 15-year-old girl, Lynda Mann, was found raped and murdered in the English countryside in 1983. Three years later, 15-year-old Dawn Ashworth was raped and murdered nearby. A 17-year-old kitchen porter confessed to the second murder but not the first; police however were convinced that both had been murdered by the same offender. The semen on both bodies had biological types that matched 10% of the population. These types also matched the accused.

The investigating police asked Professor Alec Jeffreys from the University of Leicester to analyze the samples using his new technique of 'DNA fingerprinting'. The technique had recently been publicized in the English media because it had resolved a parentage testing dispute in an immigration case (Jeffreys et al., 1986).

The semen from both deceased was concluded as having the same DNA profile – but was different to the DNA of the kitchen porter. A probability of a chance match of the DNA was determined to be smaller than 1 in 100 million (Gill and Werrett, 1987).

The world's first intelligence-led DNA screen of local men whose reference blood samples matched the initial biological screen was conducted by the Forensic Science

Service of England (a government laboratory which is now dissolved). Colin Pitchfork persuaded a work colleague to donate a sample for him, but police discovered the ruse. It was subsequently found that the DNA profile from the semen on the bodies matched Pitchfork's DNA profile. Pitchfork pleaded guilty and was sentenced for the two murders in 1988.

The paper by Professor Jeffreys and his colleagues, published in 1985, described the discovery of very variable DNA regions called 'minisatellites' (Jeffreys et al., 1985). Like many scientific findings, this variable DNA was discovered in the process of working on another problem, one in gene mapping. The 'hypervariable' DNA not only was 'hyper' variable among individuals but was also inherited in a Mendelian fashion, passed along through the generations with half from each parent. This feature is important in parentage testing, identification of deceased especially in mass disasters and comparing regions of DNA from matter on criminal exhibits.

The publicity of DNA fingerprinting fuelled the desire by the police to use the tool and was perhaps a factor in Pitchfork's initial effort to elude being tested.

The idea still used today is that a person will have a 'variable number of tandem repeats' in their own DNA. Initially, the way to analyze the repeat segments depended on having enough DNA for the steps in the process. Segments of the DNA were visualized on an x-ray film using radioactivity, depicting bands like a barcode.

Probes on large numbers of minisatellites at the same time led to multiple band patterns from multiple areas (loci, singular 'locus') on the DNA molecule. New single-locus probes were then designed that were specific to one locus.

The term 'DNA fingerprinting' has now been dropped in favour of 'DNA profiling' because of the poor analogy with fingerprints, which have no genetic statistical basis. Chapter 4 of this book describes the processes to obtain DNA and how it is interpreted.

DNA Court Challenges during Initial Implementation

The U.S. court in 1987 was one of the first to rule on the admissibility of DNA evidence (Connors et al., 1996; Scheck et al., 2000; *State v. Woodall*, 1989).

CASE 1.2   Admissibility; Evolving Science; Exclusion; Biological Link of Offences

---

Two women in West Virginia were each abducted and assaulted in separate incidents from a shopping mall car park. Glen Woodall was convicted for the two crimes and sentenced to two life terms. Biological testing of the semen samples from both cases were said to match the blood group and enzyme type of the accused, and the forensic biologist expected the traits to occur in 6 in every 10,000 males in West Virginia. Years later it was considered that this forensic interpretation was dubious.

The defence requested that a new biological test called 'DNA print analysis' be performed on these samples. No expert evidence was offered as to the reliability and validity of the technique, and the court refused to order the request.

After the trial, the prosecution agreed that DNA testing could be used by the defendant. However, there was insufficient sample to produce a result. The appeals court upheld the original convictions, but Woodall continued to pursue further DNA testing. It was subsequently agreed that DNA tests using a new copying technique (polymerase chain reaction [PCR]) could be performed on the semen samples. The samples were released for testing. It was determined that the DNA type of the accused was different to the semen from both victims – but both semen samples had the same DNA type. The state also obtained the same results and Glen Woodall was exculpated in 1992.

> An individual already serving a jail sentence was con-
> victed in a 2011 trial for these crimes – as a result of a
> DNA database hit.

The same perpetrator was identified for the two victims in Case 1.2. DNA provided a link for the forensic samples as in Case 1.1. Similarly, DNA profiling excluded the first accused man.

The copying method called polymerase chain reaction, which was used in the latter stages of Case 1.2, produces copies of target fragments of DNA. It now forms the basis of all forensic DNA typing tests.

Prior to DNA profiling, forensic scientists had low discriminatory tests available for biological matter. Until the late 1960s the only genetic markers used in forensic laboratories were the ABO blood group substances. This type of blood grouping was known to the public due to a requirement for a person to have a compatible blood type for transfusion (needed for operations, illness and accidents). Then a method for typing proteins and enzymes was found, separating out the substances in a gel. However, the biological matter often failed to yield a result because of deterioration of the particular genetic marker and could also give ambiguous results.

Mostly these tests were used as a screening tool to sift through the persons of interest and *exclude* those that did not match the crime scene sample. The first case where DNA profiling was used (Case 1.1) also relied on the initial exclusion tests using traditional biological markers.

The first case that seriously challenged the admissibility of DNA evidence was that of *People v. Joseph Castro* in the New York Supreme Court (Mnookin, 2007; *People v. Castro*, 1989).

CASE 1.3   Admissibility; Technique as Applied in the Case

A young woman and her 2-year-old daughter were found dead in their apartment in the city of New York, United States, in 1987. Both had been stabbed multiple times. The woman's partner had raised the alarm on his return to their apartment as he could not enter due to a chain locking it from the inside. He rang his mother who phoned the police. Waiting outside the building, he saw a man leaving the apartment block with blood on the face, arms and shoes. The partner later identified the man leaving as Joseph Castro, a local handyman. The police questioned Castro and noted that there appeared to be blood on his watch. They seized the watch and sent it for forensic testing.

The tests proposed that the blood found on Castro's watch had DNA that matched the DNA of the dead woman. The statistics revealed that a person, selected at random, having the same DNA profile was less than 1 in 180 million. But Castro said it was his own blood.

There was over a 3-month pretrial hearing that followed regarding the admissibility of the DNA evidence. Leading scientists stated that DNA typing was generally accepted in the scientific community. The defence contended that (1) the laboratory had failed to follow its own protocols for declaring a match, (2) forensic analysis presented different challenges to that in the research setting and (3) there were problems with the genetic database used to calculate the 'match'.

The court held that DNA was generally accepted in the scientific community but that the technique as applied in the particular case was so flawed that the evidence of a match was not admissible. However, evidence that it was *not* Castro's DNA was admissible. The court concluded that pretrial hearings are required to determine whether the testing laboratory's methods accord with scientific standards and are reliable.

The defendant pleaded guilty to the murders in late 1989 and he was never tried.

The judge wrote in his opinion: 'In a piercing attack upon each molecule of evidence presented, the defense was successful in demonstrating to this court that the testing laboratory failed in its responsibility to perform the accepted scientific techniques and experiments in several major respects.'

> It was as a result of this case that concerns were raised by the scientific and legal communities over DNA profiling in the United States. The science itself was upheld but the technique as *applied* was not.

This case was also one of the first where 'examiner bias' in DNA analysis was proposed. The defence scientist Eric Lander said there was a danger that scientists may tend to see what they are looking for when they interpret a DNA profile. A scientist could 'hallucinate a band' when they expected to see one, and a band could be discounted if it was not expected. Thus there should be tests checking any interpretations that may have been influenced by prior expectations. Chapter 9 discusses the subject of cognitive bias.

The Castro court recommended extensive discovery requirements for future proceedings including

- Copies of all laboratory results and reports
- Explanation of statistical probability calculations
- Explanations for any observed defects or laboratory errors, including observed contaminants
- Chain of custody of documents

These requirements are discovery essentials today.

The Castro case led to improved standards in forensic laboratories and motivated debate among scientists.

Pretrial hearings in English courts that decide on the admissibility of the DNA evidence were described by the 1997 court *R v. Doheny and Adams*. The risk of laboratory error, the method of DNA analysis used and the basis of subsequent statistical calculations should be examined.

Evidence Collection and Laboratory Practices

The O. J. Simpson trial focused the attention of the U.S. public on forensic evidence and DNA in particular (*People v. Simpson*, 1995).

CASE 1.4   Crime Scene and Laboratory Handling

Former football star and actor O. J. Simpson was tried on two counts of murder following the June 1994 deaths of his ex-wife Nicole Simpson and her acquaintance Ronald Goldman. The trial was held in Los Angeles, United States, from January to October in 1995. It has been described as the most publicized criminal trial in history and educated a generation of Americans on the potential of DNA evidence. It included over 100 days of televised courtroom testimony (available on the CNN website).

The defence team proposed that there was reasonable doubt about the DNA evidence, including poor internal laboratory procedures that may have contaminated the evidence and mishandling of evidence by Los Angeles police.

The accused was found not guilty.

Later in 1997 a civil suit was brought against O. J. Simpson by the family of the deceased (*Goldman v. Simpson*, 1997). The outcome was a wrongful death judgment against Simpson.

This case emphasized that collection practices of pertinent exhibits are just as important as those of the analytical process in the forensic laboratory. There needs to be confidence in all the processes used in ultimately reporting a DNA result.

Changing Technology

The science of DNA profiling is constantly evolving. Case 1.2 is an example of the advantages of using more sensitive tests.

The first DNA tests using the copying technology of PCR targeted a small number of variants on a gene and copied them many times, similar to a photocopier but a chemical process. The discriminating power was low and mixtures were difficult to interpret.

A U.S. case shows the limitations of the particular technique (Thompson et al., 2003).

CASE 1.5   Changing Technology; Exclusion

Timothy Durham was convicted for the rape of an 11-year-old girl in Oklahoma in 1993 and sentenced to 3000 years in jail. There was a claimed match between the DNA of Durham and the DNA from semen.

Further analysis found that there was an original misinterpretation of the test. There was incomplete separation of the victim's cellular material and the material from the semen. The victim's DNA type, when combined with those of the true perpetrator, produced a mixed DNA profile which was mistaken as a single-source profile matching that of Durham's.

The further tests also excluded Durham at several other genetic loci.

Durham's conviction was quashed in 1997 after serving 4 years.

The late 1990s saw the advent of short tandem repeat (STR) DNA testing. STR tests use the copying technology and also many markers on different genes. The number of markers depends on the system. The PowerPlex21 implemented in Australia in 2013 uses 21 markers.

The DNA database in England was originally developed in 1995 using a six loci system plus the sex marker (Jobling and Gill, 2004).

A DNA database match led to the arrest of a man for burglary in England (Goodwin et al., 2011)

CASE 1.6   Changing Technology; DNA Database; Exclusion

Raymond Easton was arrested in 1999 for a burglary 200 miles from his home. A profile recovered from the scene matched his DNA profile, which had been loaded onto the national DNA database as a result of a previous incident. Although he suffered from Parkinson's disease and could not drive, the police and prosecution were convinced of his guilt due to a DNA chance match of less than 1 in 37 million. During 1999 the second-generation multiplex (SGM) kit of 6 loci was changed to SGM plus with 10 loci. The chance match became less than 1 in 1 billion.

Charges were dropped against Easton when the new SGM plus kit was used on the crime sample. The four additional loci did not match the accused.

The desire to maximize the investigative potential of DNA led scientists to develop ever more sensitive methods so that genetic science could be applied to more and more casework, including 'cold cases' that had previously yielded no clues.

The first low-level or low-template technique, called low copy number (LCN), was developed by the Forensic Science Service in the United Kingdom in the late 1990s (Gill et al., 2000). This was the laboratory involved in the historic Case 1.1. LCN was viewed as a new weapon in the fight against crime. It uses extra copying in the PCR process and can achieve results from very small samples merely 'touched'.

It is now realized that many laboratories have moved into the low-template domain by improved technology – without necessarily being explicit that this is the case (Caddy et al., 2008).

A high-profile court from Northern Ireland illustrated yet again the importance of robust collection and laboratory methods (*R v. Hoey*, 2007).

CASE 1.7   Low-Level DNA; Collection Practices; Laboratory Practices; Method Validation

The Omagh bombing occurred in 1998. A car bomb killed 29 people and 220 people were injured. Sean Hoey was charged in 2005 after it was alleged his DNA was found on bomb timers collected during the crime scene examination. However, the technique of LCN did not exist in 1998. Crime scene examiners did not necessarily follow the stringent anti-contamination measures needed for such a process.

Justice Weir in the trial court of 2007 described the collection of exhibits as thoroughly disorganized and the police storage areas 'a complete mess'. The way the DNA evidence had been recovered, packaged, stored and transported was a concern. The forensic laboratory was no better, with labels routinely falling off items, and experts did not wear masks or possibly even gloves.

There was another concern about scientific opinion on the validity of the method. Justice Weir concluded that low-template DNA had not been appropriately validated by the scientific community. In his view, two articles published by the developers of the method were insufficient to validate the technique.

The accused was freed as a result of the court hearing.

Questions and concerns from this trial led the Association of Chief Police Officers to suspend the use of LCN profiling in the United Kingdom. A review by the UK Forensic Science Regulator had been commissioned prior to the case, although the findings were published a few months following the Hoey judgment. The report (Caddy et al., 2008) found that the laboratory methods were robust and fit for purpose but confusion remained in the interpretation of these kinds of profiles. The report recommended that a DNA profile using low-template DNA techniques should be presented to a jury in a criminal trial with caveats. The report also recommended further harmonization of standards for the production and interpretation of low-template DNA data.

The use of LCN DNA profiling in the United Kingdom recommenced after the Caddy review.

The final case of this chapter poses some interesting scientific (and philosophical) questions.

A U.S. man convicted of a murder was sentenced to death in 1985 (Connors et al., 1996; Innocence Project; Scheck et al., 2000). He was exonerated in 1993 after serving 8 years in jail.

CASE 1.8   Exclusion; DNA Database

Kirk Bloodsworth was convicted and sentenced to death in 1985 for the rape and murder of a 9-year-old girl in woodland in Maryland, United States, the previous year. He continued to maintain his innocence. The Maryland Court of Appeals overturned Bloodsworth's conviction in July 1986 because of information that was withheld by the prosecution. He was retried, and a jury convicted him a second time. This time Bloodsworth was sentenced to two consecutive life terms.

He read about the use of DNA profiling in a murder investigation from England (Case 1.1) in jail, and he pushed to have the evidence DNA tested. Initially, it could not be located. Eventually, the victim's semen-stained underwear was found and the semen DNA profiled. The DNA from the semen did not match the DNA of Bloodsworth. He was released from prison in 1993 although he was not formally exonerated.

In 2003, prisoner reference DNA profiles were added to state and federal DNA databases, and a crime sample match was obtained with Kimberly Shay Ruffner. A month after the murder in Maryland in 1984, Ruffner had been sentenced to 45 years for an unrelated attempted rape/murder. He was incarcerated in the same prison and a cell one floor below that of Bloodsworth.

Ruffner pleaded guilty to the 1984 murder in 2004.

Summary

The case studies in this chapter show that DNA profiling may provide a potential link with an offender using genetic technology. The cases also demonstrate that DNA profiling is a way of excluding suspects who might otherwise be falsely charged with, and convicted of, serious crimes.

Table 1.1 lists a summary of issues raised through the trials as described in this chapter.

TABLE 1.1 Summary of Issues in 'Historical' DNA Profiling
Evidence

- Improved discrimination and exclusion – Cases 1.1, 1.2, 1.5, 1.6 and 1.8
- Intelligence screen – Case 1.1
- DNA link between cases – Cases 1.1 and 1.2
- Acceptance of scientific method in the relevant community – Case 1.7
- Quality concerns regarding application of technique – Cases 1.3, 1.4 and 1.7
- Evolving technology – Cases 1.2 and 1.5 through 1.8
- DNA database – Cases 1.6 and 1.8

It often takes time for problems to be identified and awareness of limitations of practical applications of a technique. The Castro court and the Omagh bombing trial (Cases 1.3 and 1.7) illustrate that a court process could uncover limitations in evidence that scientific discourse such as publications may not reveal.

The extension of technical frontiers should also be accompanied by conceptual developments and understanding (Biedermann et al., 2014). Of course, validation of new techniques as applied in the forensic field and the particular laboratory is vital. But the implementation of new DNA profiling techniques in forensic science needs an accompanying explanation of its assumptions, limitations and meaning in the context of the case. The explanation should be in terms that an investigating officer and a courtroom without advanced scientific knowledge can understand.

The next chapters in this book will discuss the many issues involved in understanding these concepts.

References

Biedermann, A., Vuille, V. and Taroni, F. 2014. DNA, statistics and the law: A cross-disciplinary approach to forensic inference. *Front. Gen.* 5: 136.

Caddy, B., Taylor, G.R. and Linacre, A.M.T. 2008. *A Review of the Science of Low Template DNA Analysis.* Home Office Forensic Regulation Unit: U.K. Available at: https://www.gov.uk/government/publications/review-of-the-science-of-low-template-dna-analysis, accessed 25 November 2015.

Connors, E., Lundregan, T., Miller, N. et al. 1996. *Convicted by Juries: Exonerated by Science, Case Studies in the Use of DNA Evidence to Establish Innocence After Trial.* National Institute of Justice, Alexandria, Virginia. Available at: https://www.ncjrs.gov/pdffiles/dnaevid.pdf, accessed 25 November 2015.

Gill, P. and Werrett, D. 1987. Exclusion of a man charged with murder by DNA fingerprinting. *Forensic Sci. Int.* 35: 145–148.

Gill, P., Whitaker, J., Flaxman, C. et al. 2000. An investigation of the rigor of interpretation rules for STRs derived from less than 100 pg of DNA. *Forensic Sci. Int.* 112(1): 17–40.

Goldman v. Simpson. 1997. California Supreme Court of Los Angeles County. Case SC036340.

Goodwin, W., Linacre, A. and Hadi, S. 2011. *An Introduction to Forensic Genetics*, 2nd edn. John Wiley & Sons Ltd: Chichester, U.K.

Innocence Project. Available at: http://www.innocenceproject.org, accessed 25 November 2015.

Jeffreys, A.J., Brookfield, J. and Semeonoff, R. 1986. Positive identification of an immigration test case using DNA fingerprints. *Nature* 317: 818–819.

Jeffreys, A.J., Wilson, V. and Thein, S.L. 1985. Hypervariable minisatellite regions in human DNA. *Nature* 314: 67–73.

Jobling, M. and Gill, P. 2004. Encoded evidence: DNA in forensic analysis. *Nat. Rev. Gen.* 5: 739–751.

Mnookin, J.L. 2007. People v Castro: Challenging the forensic use of DNA profiling evidence. *J. Scholarly Perspect.* 3: 01.

National Research Council. 2009. *Strengthening Forensic Science in the United States: A Path Forward*. National Academy Press: Washington, DC.

People v. Castro. 1989. 144 Misc. NYS 2d 956.

People v. Simpson. 1995. California Supreme Court of Los Angeles County. Case BA097211.

R v. Doheny and Adams. 1997. 1 Criminal Appeals R 369 England.

R v. Hoey. 2007. The Crown Court sitting in Northern Ireland. NICC 49.

Scheck, B., Neufeld, P. and Dwyer, J. 2000. *Actual Innocence*. Doubleday: New York.

State of West Virginia v Glen Dale Woodall. 1989. Supreme Court of Appeals. No. 18662 July 6. Available at: http://law.justia.com/cases/west-virginia/supreme-court/1989/18662-5.html, accessed 25 November 2015.

Thompson, W.C., Taroni, F. and Aitken, C.G.G. 2003. How the probability of a false positive affects the value of DNA evidence. *J. Forensic Sci.* 48: 1–8.

Wambaugh, J. 1989. *The Blooding*. William Morrow: New York.

Chapter 2

Context

Introduction

DNA profiling is a powerful discriminating tool. The previous chapter has shown its effectiveness in the investigation process.

The context of the DNA result is paramount. DNA alone will not exonerate or incriminate. It is the interpretation of that DNA in the context of the case that may do so. Furthermore, the DNA result(s) may not necessarily extend to the prosecution arena.

A DNA result may be obtained from a stain or a deposit of biological material. Numerous DNA results may be obtained from a forensic examination, from different exhibits and from different deposits on the same exhibit. There may be different contributors to one deposit, resulting in mixture DNA profiles.

The DNA evidence from an exhibit in a criminal case may support the hypothesis or scenario proposed, or it may not. The evidence could be equivocal – neither hypothesis is supported or refuted.

A DNA result may be compromised through the scientific processes that yielded it or through the interpretation of its meaning in the context of the case. Chapter 9 discusses quality concerns regarding the result. This chapter addresses the context.

The *scientific method* explicitly considers alternative hypotheses when conducting an experiment. The investigator – for example a medical or a scientific researcher – seeks to determine the solution of a problem from a variety of causes. What may cause a particular disease, what may not? Could it be genetic or transmitted?

Alternative scenarios are considered by the crime investigator questioning the case – who may have committed the crime, why and how. Various scenarios other than the one proposed are debated during investigatory stages of a crime.

The court tests the prosecution scenario and the alternative defence scenario, and the judge(s) and/or jury are involved in the decision-making process. Part of the quality control system of the judicial process is the rigorous testing.

Alternate hypothesis of the meaning of the DNA in the context of the case is considered as in any scientific examination. The forensic analysis incorporates the scientific method at each stage, from the initial unveiling of the exhibit to its sampling and evaluation (Taupin and Cwiklik, 2010).

A single DNA result may contradict all the other evidence. A prosecution and trial in Australia used DNA not only to convict but also as the only evidence that a crime was committed at all (Vincent, 2010).

CASE 2.1   Single DNA Result; Database Match; Contradiction; Contamination

An unconscious woman was found in a bathroom cubicle at a nightclub in 2006. She could not remember what had happened, and the police conveyed her to a hospital for a medical examination. The samples from the woman arrived in the forensic laboratory as an 'unknown offender' case. A DNA profile was obtained from one medical swab, and there were spermatozoa on the associated microscope smear (1 intact spermatozoa and 15 sperm heads). No other samples were positive. This DNA 'matched' via a database hit the DNA of

Farah Jama, a 19-year-old man. It was concluded by the forensic scientist that it was 800 billion times more likely that the DNA originated from Jama than if it originated from another person. There was no other evidence. Farah Jama was convicted at trial in 2008, sentenced to 6 years jail, and served 15 months in prison.

The conviction was overturned on appeal in December 2009. It was realized that samples from an unrelated sexual incident involving Jama, where no charges were eventually laid, were taken by the same medical officer at the same location within 30 hours of medical samples from the alleged rape victim.

An inquiry was initiated when it was clear that there had been a miscarriage of justice resulting in wrongful conviction and imprisonment. It was found that DNA evidence had been the only link between Farah Jama and the unconscious woman. The report tabled in the state parliament found that the offence probably never happened. Most likely contamination between the evidentiary samples occurred in the medical exami-nation although the exact mechanism could not be determined.

The conclusion of the inquiry stated that the DNA evidence was perceived to appear so powerful by all involved in the case that none of the filters on which our criminal justice system depends to minimize the risk of a miscarriage of justice operated effectively at any stage, until a matter of weeks before Jama's appeal. The unreserved acceptance of the reliability of the DNA evidence appeared to have so confined thought that it enabled all involved to leap over a veritable mountain of improbabilities and unexplained aspects that could be seen to block the path to conviction. No one appeared to be aware of the dangers of relying on statistical prob-abilities in the determination of guilt.

The inquiry stated 'it is almost incredible that, in consequence of a minute particle, so small that it was invisible to the naked eye, being released into the environment and settling on a swab, slide or trolley surface, a chain of events could be started that culminated in the conviction of an individual for a crime that had never been committed by him or anyone else, created immense personal distress for many people and exposed a number of deficiencies in our criminal justice system. But that, I believe, is what happened' (Vincent, 2010).

The recommendations of the report included education of legal practitioners and members of the judiciary on the nature and appropriate use of DNA.

If the assumptions or limitations are not described in forensic reports or testimony, then these may not be understood. There is a responsibility for the scientist to place the evidence in context and to point out the limitations of interpretation (see, for example, Taupin and Cwiklik, 2010; Vincent, 2010). Limitations of the DNA result(s) in any case should be conveyed in *both* the report and testimony of the forensic scientist.

Evidence, including DNA results, can arise in three broad ways:

1. Innocent means
2. The crime event
3. Contamination or inadvertent transfer

The mechanism of transfer of a DNA profile is a consideration for every case reported. That is, how has the DNA been transferred to the exhibit in question? Chapter 3 discusses DNA transfer.

Controversies over legal cases such as the murder of Meredith Kercher in Italy reveal that there are still difficulties in understanding the meaning of a DNA profiling result in context. This case is discussed later in this chapter and other chapters as it illustrates many issues.

The extension of technical frontiers should also be accompanied by conceptual developments and understandings (for example, Champod, 2013). The improved discriminatory power provided by DNA profiling may have a paradoxical effect. The test is a valued technique and used in a widespread manner. Conversely, there could be the belief that the test result is all important and the context irrelevant.

Exhibits in Context

Sometimes the most pertinent exhibits are not examined, or there may be insufficient results. The possibility of other exhibits that may have been collected by the police and not tested by the forensic laboratory should be considered.

Although adjudicated some time ago, Case 2.2 illustrates issues that are relevant today. DNA evidence, and indeed any scientific evidence, should not be used solely as a prosecutorial tool. It may be more important to consider the DNA as an investigatory tool to *exclude* suspects.

This case also illustrates the failure to consider all items submitted to the laboratory in the context of the case (*Queen v. Button*, 2001).

CASE 2.2   Insufficient Examination;
Investigation versus Prosecution; Exclusion

A girl was assaulted in Australia in 1999 and nominated Frank Button as the offender. There were spermatozoa obtained from an intimate medical swab, but no DNA profile could be obtained. Sheets and pillowcases from the girl's bedding were also sent to the laboratory but not tested. Button was convicted and sentenced to 7 years of imprisonment.

His appeal was heard on the grounds that there was no scientific evidence presented at the trial. The laboratory tested the bedding on insistence from the defence lawyers. The DNA profile from the semen on the bedding did not match the DNA profile of Button. The laboratory then retested the medical swabs and obtained a DNA profile that again did not match Frank Button but matched the male profile on the sheets. The medical swab profile matched that of a convicted offender on the DNA database, and Frank Button was acquitted. The Queensland Court of Appeal noted that DNA testing should not only be used to identify a perpetrator of a crime but also to exclude suspects from an investigation.

It is always worthwhile to investigate further if it is thought the original police exhibits, such as clothing from the victim, have been destroyed. Medical swabs or debris collected from the items may still remain in case files or exhibit rooms or refrigerators. The stability of DNA, whether nuclear or mitochondrial, means there is a potential for obtaining a result of evidential value many years later from the date of the original crime.

Medical examination kits comprising intimate swabs from a complainant in a sexual offence may still remain on exhibit shelves in storerooms. The U.S. government funding was originally provided in 2004 to address the backlog of medical kits in that country. The 'Debbie Smith Backlog Grant Program', reauthorized in 2014, provides federal government grants to conduct DNA analysis of the backlogged samples (H.R.4323 113th Congress 2014). The Debbie Smith Act was initially authorized in 2004 as part of the 'Justice For All Act of 2004' (P.L. 108–145). The namesake of this act and her case are summarized.

CASE 2.3   Untested Exhibits; DNA Database

A man wearing a ski mask intruded into Debbie Smith's home in Virginia in 1989. He dragged her to the woods and sexually assaulted her. She had a medical examination and intimate medical swabs were obtained. These were not tested until 1994, some 5 years later. A male DNA profile was obtained and placed on the DNA database in 1995. Norman Jimmerson was identified and sentenced to 161 years in prison for the crime.

The rape kit backlog still exists in the United States at the time of writing, and Debbie Smith still petitions for action (Augenstein, 2015).

The intervening years between an offence and the testing of pertinent exhibits may leave an offender free to commit further crimes. These lost years may also cause distress to the complainant when medical samples (obtained under confronting conditions) remain unexamined and thus no scientific corroboration to their story.

Furthermore, the testing may identify another perpetrator when there has been a person prosecuted on other evidence – and exclude that person (Cases 2.2 and 2.5).

Context of Testing

There may be alternative explanations for the biological evidence, and consequently the DNA evidence. Case 2.4 (from the case files of the author) shows the importance of considering alternate scenarios for the deposition of the biological fluid.

CASE 2.4   Deposition of Matter; Alternate Scenarios; Correlation

It was alleged that a care worker sexually assaulted a mentally impaired woman. A medical examination kit and underpants from the woman were submitted to the forensic laboratory. There was no semen from the medical samples, but semen was detected on the underpants. There was one semen stain with spermatozoa detected and a presumptive semen stain detected. Both stains were to the upper back, just below the waistband, of the garment. The DNA from the confirmed semen stain matched the DNA of the accused. The DNA from the presumptive semen stain was a mixture that corresponded to at least three contributors.

Vaginal discharge of semen after penile–vaginal intercourse may be found on the inner crotch area of the underwear worn after the event. The confirmed semen stain on the upper back of the underpants in this case was circular in shape and discrete, while the presumptive semen stain was also discrete and a 'mirror image' of the other.

One hypothesis as to the deposition of the seminal stain was that there was direct ejaculation of semen onto the material of the garment. Another hypothesis was that the area of the garment contacted an object coated with wet semen so that semen was transferred to the fabric. It was also considered that the 'mirror image' stain may have occurred through a transfer of fluid during folding of the garment when wet, but was insufficient to transfer any spermatozoa. The alleged event occurred in a bathroom and wet and diluted surfaces may have contacted the fabric.

The judge at trial did not admit the DNA evidence as it was deemed more prejudicial than probative. The prosecution discontinued proceedings.

Depending on the age and condition and subsequent to any washing, clothing may act like a 'reservoir' of DNA (Taupin and Cwiklik, 2010). The modes of deposition of liquid or dried biological material on fabric, indeed any surface, should be considered. Some surfaces may readily absorb and retain liquid material as the liquid acts as a ready vector, but dried material such as dried blood, semen, saliva or skin cells can also be transferred to a surface by mechanisms such as abrasion and be incorporated within the material.

Issues such as secondary transfer should also be considered. It is possible that biological fluid and thus DNA from a person can be deposited via intermediary object(s) (indirect transfer).

If matter is denoted as a particular biological fluid, such as semen from an intimate medical sample – and a DNA profile is obtained from it – alternate hypotheses can be proposed. One hypothesis is that the semen came from the perpetrator. Contamination can also be a hypothesis.

One hypothesis proposed by the prosecution in one of the numerous proceedings against the accused contradicted the rationale traditionally used in sexual offence cases. This case follows (Innocence Project; Martin, 2011).

CASE 2.5   DNA Database; Exclusion

During 1992 in the United States, an 11-year-old girl was murdered. Holly Staker was babysitting two younger children – 2 and 5 years old. Juan Rivera was convicted for the murder in 1993. He was 19 years old at the time and had previously been convicted of burglary and was on home monitoring. He had a further two trials, each after an appeal, and was convicted each time. Before the third trial in 2009, there was DNA testing of the semen found inside the deceased. This DNA eliminated Rivera as the source of the semen. An appellate court in 2011 ruled that the conviction could not stand. Juan Rivera was released from prison in 2012.

The police and prosecutors had explained the DNA from the semen by theorizing that Holly was sexually active – the semen came from consensual sex shortly before her murder.

Clinging to one scenario over any others, despite evidence to the contrary, is not part of the scientific method. The principles of the scientific method are discussed at the end of this chapter.

Association with a Body Fluid/Matter

DNA may be linked to a stain or deposit of biological material, for example, semen or blood. However, it is not possible to infer from a DNA sample profile alone that the DNA came from a particular body fluid origin.

Presumptive tests for a biological fluid, by their very definition, are not confirmatory tests. If it is required to confirm blood, semen, or saliva in a sample, confirmatory tests should be performed.

Table 2.1 depicts a summary of biological screening tests. Table 2.2 depicts confirmatory tests.

The consequences of denoting a stain as a particular fluid such as blood using presumptive testing – and not confirmatory – were graphically illustrated nearly 30 years ago in the 'dingo' case from Australia. Baby Azaria disappeared from a campsite near Uluru (Ayers Rock) in the desert of central Australia in 1980. Lindy Chamberlain said that a dingo (a wild dog) took her baby from their tent. She was convicted at trial of murdering her baby inside her car and sentenced to life imprisonment. Her husband

TABLE 2.1 Biological Screening Tests

Blood

- Hemastix test strips
- Luminol test using chemiluminescence
- Phenolpthalein tests using colour reactions

Semen

- Alternative light sources
- Test for acid phosphatase present in seminal fluid
- Prostate specific antigen (PSA) or P30 present in high amounts in seminal fluid

Saliva

- Alternative light sources
- Phadebas test for salivary amylase

Skin cells – No test available

TABLE 2.2 Biological Confirmatory Tests

Blood

- Hemachromogen reagent producing crystals visualised under microscope
- Antihuman hemoglobin tests with 'lines of identity'

Semen

- Identification of sperm
- Immunodiffusion tests with antibodies, possible false positives

Saliva

- Immunodiffusion tests with antibodies, false positives noted

Skin cells – No test available

was convicted of being an accessory to murder and given a suspended prison sentence. The child was never found. A few years later, there was an Australian Royal Commission that enquired into these convictions (Morling, 1987). The commission found that the test used to denote that there was blood from a baby inside a car was not specific and gave a positive result to 'sound deadener' used as a coating inside the car. The convictions were vacated. Lindy Chamberlain had served 4 years in prison. A final coronial inquest in 2012 found that, indeed, a dingo had taken Lindy Chamberlain's baby (Morris, 2012).

Although not the first option, it may be possible to go back and retest the deposit to confirm that the material was from a particular biological somatic origin.

Current forensic laboratory tests cannot show that a DNA deposit is from skin cells. It also cannot be assumed that touched objects contain only low amounts of DNA from the skin cells. Objects that are simply touched may contain quantities that may be encountered from blood or semen stains. It is the quality of the DNA that is important. Blood or semen deposits may be degraded or inhibited and produce poor quality DNA profiles.

DNA alone cannot be related to a specific action. DNA profiles obtained from an object may have been deposited at separate times/places to the event in question if their body location cannot be determined. DNA from an unspecified cellular source reduces the relevance of biological evidence to a particular event and increases the uncertainty as to how the DNA may have been transferred to the item.

One bizarre case where a type of biological fluid was assumed from one event, and then results of this used to prosecute a suspect for another event, follows (from the author's case files).

CASE 2.6   Biological Fluid not Denoted; Statistical Conflict

Occupants in a house heard a man outside in the street make a grunting noise. They looked out the window and saw a crouched figure in the darkness.

It was alleged that about an hour later a partly naked male stranger intruded into the bedroom of a woman in a nearby house. She stated this man moved towards her with a pillow from her home, as if to suffocate, and she fell on the floor. She then ran outside into the street and alerted security.

The next day, crime scene investigators were called and observed a deposit outside the first premises and collected it with a swab; later this swab was submitted for forensic analysis. The fabric covering of the pillow from the alleged assault was submitted for DNA analysis.

Tests for semen were negative from the swab. A 'differential extraction' was performed on the swab; this type of extraction is usually performed on a medical swab from a female to isolate sperm from the female material. It was reported that the 'sperm fraction' from the swab (although no sperm was identified) had a partial male DNA profile with components matching a full male DNA profile obtained from the 'non-sperm fraction'. The full male DNA profile was placed on the DNA database and matched an individual deemed to be the perpetrator in the assault. Sexual proclivity was inferred for this person despite no support for semen – on any items.

There were at least three contributors to the DNA from four areas of the fabric over the pillow; the complainant was excluded. Initial tests included the accused as one of the three contributors with a large statistical weighting. Further testing before the trial determined there were at least four contributors to the fabric. A statistical weighting calculation could not be performed for this number of contributors.

Charges were dropped before trial.

Different fractions obtained during a differential extraction separation for sperm do not confirm that a sample is from the semen. Identifying sperm is the only method for confirming semen. If there is a suspected semen stain and this is not from an internal medical swab from a female or her intimate clothing, then assuming a mixture of individuals is not the first option.

There is progress for confirmatory tests for body fluid origin. Smaller amounts of sample may be used for confirmatory tests and in a manner where it is collected in the same sample as that extracted for DNA. This is to try and obtain as much DNA as possible from the sample and not compromise the quality or quantity. Markers (messenger RNA) in body fluid have been investigated.

Mixture DNA profiles are problematic in that a mixture of body fluids may exist in the one stain producing mixture DNA profiles. A particular body fluid, or mixtures of such, cannot be determined from a DNA profile alone. Mixture DNA profiles may have a major contribution from cellular material and a minor contribution from the blood, or vice versa.

Staged approaches are recommended to collect samples if mixtures of matter are predicted. For example analyzing a material underneath the fingernails from a victim where foreign material is suspected – and there may be blood – requires consideration of mixture sampling. An attempt to minimize donor DNA and maximize foreign DNA can be employed. Blood staining may originate from the fingernail donor themselves due to the blood-letting that resulted from the event.

A staged approach to mixtures from intimate medical swabs in sexual assault cases has been used since the forensic inception of DNA (Gill et al., 1985; Case 1.1). 'Differential lysis' is used to isolate sperm from female cellular material. Sometimes, even today, this separation is incomplete or unsuccessful. There may be mixtures of DNA from both parties in the one fraction.

Time of Deposition

The time that the DNA was deposited may be the ultimate issue. How the DNA got on the exhibit, and whether that DNA is relevant to the offence, may be in question. Increasingly, issues regarding transfer of trace amounts of DNA are debated in criminal proceedings. Transfer issues are further discussed in Chapter 3.

A case follows of a shooting ambush in Northern Ireland illustrating the issues involved in relating DNA found on an item to an event such as the crime. There were two trials in a 'Diplock' court (judge without jury) and one intervening appeal (*Queen v. Duffy and Shivers*, 2012; *Queen v. Shivers*, 2013).

CASE 2.7   Time of Deposit; Trace DNA; Contamination; Low Level

Two hooded gunmen emerged from a car and killed two off-duty soldiers outside the Massereene army barracks in March 2009. Two other soldiers and two pizza delivery men were shot in a burst of fire from automatic rifles.

After the shooting, it was believed that the gunmen got into the front passenger and back seats of the car. A few hours later in countryside, a partially burnt abandoned car was found; this car was agreed as that used in the attack. An Irish republican paramilitary group the 'Real Irish Republican Army' claimed the responsibility.

The core of the prosecution case was circumstantial and concerned DNA obtained from items in the car (and from the road near the car) that contained trace amounts. The tip of a latex glove found in the front footwell of the car had a full DNA profile matching that of Colin Duffy. Swabs were taken from the passenger side of the car, seat belt buckle, the interior of a mobile phone and the struck matchstick from the road. Initial examination of these items by an English laboratory determined that all three samples were mixtures containing very little DNA (low level).

A U.S. commercial computer system 'TrueAllele' was used to provide a statistical weighting. This computer program uses a so-called fully continuous model using peak heights, discussed further in Chapter 5. It was reported that a match between the seat buckle and Duffy was six trillion times more probable than coincidence. It was also reported that the match between the mobile phone and Shivers was six billion times more probable than coincidence and between the matchstick outside the car and Shivers was one million times more probable (Perlin and Galloway, 2012; Thompson et al., 2012).

The admissibility of this DNA evidence was challenged at the trial of Duffy and Shivers. The prosecution experts stated that 'TrueAllele' was based on generally accepted scientific methods with validation studies published in peer review journals. The judge could not exercise his discretion based on the testimony to exclude the DNA evidence and admitted it.

The judge in the first trial (*Queen v. Duffy and Shivers*) was satisfied that the DNA found on the glove was from Duffy and also the DNA on the passenger seat belt buckle. However, this could not provide a link to the murder. Shivers was convicted on January 2012, and Duffy was acquitted since his role in the murders was not proven. The judge said Shivers was deemed to be a secondary party to the killings, responsible for making a failed effort to burn out the getaway car.

Shivers' conviction was quashed by the Northern Ireland Court of Appeal in January 2013, and in May 2013, a retrial found him not guilty.

The prosecution case was that the DNA of Shivers was on three exhibits that pointed conclusively to him setting fire to the vehicle and/or conveying the culprits away.

The DNA results were re-examined by the first English laboratory. There had been another two struck matchsticks found on the back seat of the car. It was discovered that a crime scene examiner had lowered the back seat of the car onto these matches during the search of the car. These matchsticks had also been sitting in the car for 4 days and were then collected and placed in the same bag.

The DNA from the mobile phone showed at least three and perhaps up to five individuals in a mixture.

At a late stage in the trial, it was revealed that the DNA of a crime scene investigator was on the car key. The judge said that this showed that the investigator's claim he did not touch the key was not true or that it demonstrated the ease with which DNA can be transferred even by an experienced crime scene investigator wearing gloves.

A full DNA profile of the tower of the car to the forensic garage was found on the hand brake and gear lever.

The judge found that he could not be sure that the DNA found on the matchsticks and the mobile phone could not have got there by 'innocent transfer'. The judge said he had asked himself whether the prosecution had eliminated other possibilities, as they were obliged to do, and he was not satisfied beyond reasonable doubt that they had. Shivers was immediately released from jail.

Context, transfer, low-level DNA, contamination and statistics were all issues raised in this case. This case had many DNA issues in common with another Northern Ireland matter, *R v. Hoey*, 2007 (Case 1.7).

The murder of a British exchange student in Italy was high profile around the world, and the trials and appeals also cover many issues (Balding, 2013; Gill, 2014).

CASE 2.8   Time of Deposit; Contamination; Low Level

A 21-year-old Meredith Kercher was stabbed to death in Perugia, Italy, in 2007. She was found in her own bedroom in the apartment she shared with three other girls, including Amanda Knox. The deceased was found on the floor with throat stab wounds and was sexually assaulted, and later it was discovered some of her belongings had been stolen. Rudy Guede was convicted in 2008 of murdering and sexually assaulting Meredith Kercher and sentenced to 30 years in jail, reduced to 16 years on appeal in December 2009. The evidence against Guede appeared to be uncontroversial with DNA profiles matching his DNA profile on Kercher's body and clothing.

The DNA evidence against Knox and her boyfriend Sollecito was from a knife found at Sollecito's flat in a kitchen drawer and bra clasps from the victim at the crime scene. Knox was sentenced to 26 years in prison and Sollecito to 25 years, in December 2009.

The knife allegedly had traces of DNA matching Amanda Knox on the handle and DNA matching Meredith Kercher on the blade. The DNA alleged to have come from Knox was not disputed (it was her boyfriend's flat), but the DNA profile alleged to have come from Kercher was very-low-level DNA. There was no evidence that this low-level profile was from the blood. The suspects and victim knew each other and had access to each other's apartments. Questions were raised about handling and packaging.

This case is illustrative of the prosecution inferring the association of an *activity* such as *stabbing* with a DNA profile that could not be sourced to a particular time or body fluid.

This case also demonstrates the many factors that need to be considered in the collection, handling, and interpretation of DNA evidence, including low level or small amounts of DNA (see Chapter 6 for a discussion on low-level DNA including this case).

Scientific Method

Scientific principles and practices are employed in forensic science to obtain results that the courts expect are reliable.

Forensic science is the science applied to matters of the law. Forensic derives from the Latin 'of or before the forum'. The forum was a public space during the ancient Roman Republic and Roman Empire. Members of the public would hear and present a criminal case.

The discipline of science is defined by the notion of hypothesis testing. First, a hypothesis, or theory, is proposed. Experiments are then performed to test this hypothesis. The results of the experiments will either support or refute the hypothesis (or be equivocal). The scientific method provides the framework for the testing of the hypothesis. There should always be alternative hypotheses considered in a forensic science examination (Taupin and Cwiklik, 2010).

A letter from Einstein to a colleague demonstrates the importance of a holistic approach to science and a consideration of context. He wrote, '...I fully agree with you about the significance and educational value of methodology as well as history and philosophy of science. So many people today – and even professional scientists – seem to me like someone who has seen thousands of trees but has never seen a forest...' (Einstein, 1944).

Appropriate data in support of a conclusion should be made available in the form of publicly available (and usually published) validation studies. The forensic scientist should be conversant with relevant specialist literature, *including criticism*.

The scientific method incorporates reproducibility, rigour, transparency and independent verification. This is all part of a quality system. Quality is further discussed in Chapter 9.

References

Augenstein, S. 2015. Rape kit backlog could get mandatory testing, congressional panel says. *Forensic Magazine*, 21 May 2015. Digital version available at: http://www.forensicmag.com/articles/2015/05/rape-kit-backlog-could-get-mandatory-testing-congressional-panel-says, accessed 25 November 2015.

Balding, D. 2013. Evaluation of mixed source low template DNA profiles in forensic science. *Proc. Natl. Acad. Sci. USA* 110(30): 12241–12246.

Champod, C. 2013. DNA transfer: Informed judgement or mere guesswork. *Front. Genet.* 4: 300.

Einstein, A. 1944. Letter to Robert A. Thornton. Einstein Archive. December EA-674. Hebrew University: Jerusalem, Israel.

Gill, P. 2014. *Misleading DNA Evidence: Reasons for Miscarriages of Justice.* Academic Press: London, U.K.

Gill, P., Jeffreys, A. and Werrett, D.J. 1985. Forensic application of DNA 'fingerprinting'. *Nature* 318: 577–579.

Inquest into the death of Azaria Chamberlain, 12 June 2012, NTMC 020. Coroner's Court Darwin Australia Judgement D107/80. Available online at: http://www.nt.gov.au/justice/courtsupp/coroner/findings/other/chamberlain_findings.pdf, accessed 21 November 2015.

Martin, A. 2011. The prosecution case against DNA. *New York Times Magazine*, 27 November 2011. Page MM4, Sunday Magazine also available at http://www.nytimes.com/2011/11/27/magazine/dna-evidence-lake-county.html, accessed 25 November 2015.

Perlin, M.W. and Galloway, J. 2012. Computer DNA evidence interpretation in the real IRA Massereene terrorist attack. *Evid. Technol. Mag.* 10(3): 20–23.

Queen v. Brian Patrick Shivers. 3 May 2013. NICC 10. Available at: http://www.courtsni.gov.uk/en-GB/Judicial%20Decisions/PublishedByYear/Documents/2013/[2013]%20NICC%2010/j_j_DEE8805Final.htm, accessed 21 November 2013.

Queen v. Duffy and Shivers. 20 January 2012. NICC 37 and NICC 1. Available at: https://www.courtsni.gov.uk/en-GB/Judicial%20Decisions/Summary Judgments/Documents/Summary%20of%20judgment%20-%20R%20v%20Duffy%20and%20Shivers/j_sj_R-v-Duffy-and-Shivers_200112.html, accessed 21 November 2015.

Queen v. Frank Allan Button. 10 April 2001. Queensland Court of Criminal Appeal, QCA 133.

Royal Commission of Inquiry into Chamberlain Convictions. Morling T. 1987 Report. Commonwealth of Australia Parliamentary Papers, Vol. 15, paper 192.

SWGAM Scientific Working Group on DNA Analysis Methods. 2014. Guidelines for the Collection and Serological Examination of Biological Evidence. Available at: http://www.swgdam.org/, accessed 22 November 2015.

Taupin, J.M. and Cwiklik, C. 2010. *Scientific Protocols for Forensic Examination of Clothing.* CRC Press: Boca Raton, FL.

Thompson, W.C., Mueller, D. and Krane, D. 2012. Forensic DNA statistics: Still controversial in some cases. *The Champion*, 36(10): 12–23 December 2012.

Vincent, H.F. 2010. Inquiry into the circumstances that led to the conviction of Mr Farah Abdulkadir Jama. Victorian Government Printer: Melbourne, Victoria, Australia.

Chapter **3**

Transfer

Introduction

One of the most important investigative and court questions concerning DNA evidence may be as follows: 'how did the DNA arrive on this exhibit?' Cases from the previous chapters have asked this very question. However, the knowledge regarding DNA transfer has not kept pace with technological advances to interpret ever smaller amounts of DNA.

'Trace DNA' ─(defined in this book as DNA that cannot be related to a specific biological fluid/matter)─ is problematic. There is an increase in the degree of uncertainty as to how the DNA may have been transferred, and the relevance of findings may be difficult to assess. This chapter discusses the transfer of 'trace DNA'.

What has previously been accepted as a 'truism' in DNA transfer or logically acceptable by the lay person may indeed *not* be so according to the latest forensic science literature.

The High Court of Australia recently recognized the possibility of DNA transferring through another way than *directly* from the person of interest. Furthermore, the time of the DNA deposit was not determined. The item in question was a 'didgeridoo', an indigenous Australian musical instrument (*Fitzgerald v. The Queen*, 2014; *Queen v. Sumner and Fitzgerald*, 2013).

CASE 3.1 Transfer of DNA; Time of Deposit; Social Contact

A man died and another had brain injuries from a violent altercation in the south of Australia in 2011. A group of men forced their way into a home and attacked two of the occupants using weapons, including axes and gardening forks. The trial before a judge and jury convicted Grant Sumner and Daniel Fitzgerald for murder, and both were sentenced to life imprisonment.

There was no direct evidence that either man inflicted the fatal injury or injuries. The prosecution of Daniel Fitzgerald relied on DNA obtained from a didgeridoo. It was proposed that the DNA on the didgeridoo derived from Fitzgerald's blood and was transferred at the time of the attack. The defence argued that alternative hypotheses regarding the deposition of DNA were open. These hypotheses included a handshake between Fitzgerald and Sumner the previous evening at a social event.

On the night in question, the man that was now deceased had played the didgeridoo. At some point it was then leaning on a freezer in the kitchen, and it was briefly picked up by one of the occupants of the house to defend herself during the attack. The musical instrument finally ended up in the living room next to the deceased, and it was stained with what appeared to be blood.

The didgeridoo was alleged to have several DNA deposits – DNA matching that of the deceased, the other victim and several unknown people. There was DNA obtained from two tiny reddish-brown spots. These spots were not examined in situ for blood pattern appearance (blood pattern analysis). In fact, the reporting scientist had never seen the didgeridoo, only photographs. The samples had been scraped off by others and then submitted for biological examination.

The prosecution submitted that it was open for the jury to conclude the method of deposition of the spots was airborne due to their very small size – as opposed to transfer or contact.

There were large areas of reddish-brown staining on the didgeridoo with DNA that matched the DNA of the deceased and the other victim. The prosecution submitted that this inferred there was blood from the two tiny spots. The stains on the didgeridoo alleged to be blood were not confirmed as blood – the test was positive for a blood screening test only. It was said by the prosecution scientist that blood is a rich source of DNA. By way of contrast, trace DNA contact through skin cells is a very poor source of DNA.

If the red spots were not blood, it was necessary to consider whether the DNA came from direct transfer or secondary transfer. The hypothesis of a handshake required secondary transfer. The scientist stated primary transfer was a much more likely source of DNA than that of secondary transfer. DNA matching that of Fitzgerald provided the major component of the DNA mixture from the stain. The DNA matching that of Sumner was not in the stain. Secondary transfer was thus unlikely as the direct depositor of the DNA did not leave any of their own DNA behind. However, the scientist noted that DNA could not be 'dated'.

At the appeal in South Australia, the supreme court dismissed the defence transfer scenario of a handshake with the convicted man the previous night. The court decided that it was a 'succession of unlikely events' for the DNA of Fitzgerald to be transferred by secondary transfer. The conviction was reaffirmed.

The High Court of Australia in 2014 allowed an appeal against this decision. The high court ruled that the recovery of the appellant's DNA did not raise any inference about the time when the DNA was deposited or the circumstances in which it was deposited. The prosecution could not establish beyond reasonable doubt that the appellant was present at, and participated

> in, the attack. The high court directed that a verdict of
> acquittal be entered.

This case raises many issues. The following are findings in the
scientific literature:

- Forensic examination of a stain or deposit requires the
  scientific method and includes evaluation of morphology,
  location and extent.
- A sampling decision can then be scientifically informed.
- Biological confirmatory tests are required to denote blood.
- All biological tests consume sample, including presump-
  tive tests.
- A DNA profile cannot inform as to how it was transferred.
- A DNA profile cannot inform as to its time of deposit.
- The amount of DNA cannot inform as to its body origin
  (such as blood).
- The absence of a person's DNA in a mixed profile cannot
  imply that the person did not transfer the DNA.

If the deposit or stain is not initially scientifically evaluated, then
the context may be lost. A lack of initial evaluation may impact on
the resulting quality of the DNA profile. Mixtures of DNA from
two or more people and what is termed low level or small amounts
of DNA introduce further complicating factors in the interpretation of a DNA profile.

Principles of DNA Transfer

Factors that affect the findings of DNA on items or surfaces are
transfer, persistence and detection. While *detection* methods have
improved with advancing technology, studies regarding *transfer*
and *persistence* have not kept pace.

The concepts of divisible matter and transfer relate to the
generation of evidence. Other concepts relate to the recognition, analysis and interpretation of evidence (Inman and Rudin,
2002). A forensic science examination of exhibits should incorporate an understanding of all these concepts (Taupin and
Cwiklik, 2010).

Different levels of transfer of trace material such as glass, paint, hairs and fibres have long been recognized. Primary, secondary and tertiary transfer has been discussed. Levels of trace evidence transfer of fibres were examined in a casework context by this author (Taupin, 1996); case follows.

CASE 3.2   Levels of Trace Transfer; Primary, Secondary and Tertiary

A girl was allegedly abducted in a car and rape attempted by the accused driver who denied any contact. Clothing and the covers from the front seats of the car were analyzed for trace evidence. Synthetic fibres similar to those composing the car seat covers were located on the victim's clothing, possibly through direct transfer. Secondary transfer was indicated by dyed-brown human head-type hairs (possibly originating from the wife of the accused) located on the car seat covers and the victim's clothing. Secondary and even tertiary transfer was indicated by pink synthetic material comprising both small sections of fabric and fibres (possibly originating from the victim's mother) located on the victim's clothing, the car seat cover and the clothing of the accused. Exemplars could not be obtained from the wife of the accused nor for the pink synthetic material. The mother of the victim was a piece work machinist for clothing manufacturers and worked from home.

Secondary transfer was defined in the case as the first indirect transfer of fibres after a primary or direct transfer, taking place via an intermediary object, and may be followed by a tertiary or higher transfer. Different modes of transfer were postulated in the case.

The study of secondary transfer of fibres had previously focused on its role in contamination, especially when misinterpreted as evidence of direct contact. However, this case showed the value of considering secondary and higher levels of transfer of fibres in context.

The existence of tertiary transfer of gunshot residue (GSR) has recently been confirmed (French and Morgan, 2015). Particles may be deposited on the hands of an individual who is standing in the proximity of a discharge but who has not fired the weapon. The authors state that alternative means of GSR deposition must be acknowledged when interpreting the presence of GSR on a surface or object. The importance of secondary and tertiary transfer when reconstructing firearm incidents is stressed.

The transfer of visible (at least by the naked eye) deposits of biological matter has different considerations to that of the transfer of non-visible deposits. The morphology of blood spatter stains or semen stains on clothing, for example, may provide additional information on the method of deposition (Taupin and Cwiklik, 2010).

The principles of transfer of *trace* DNA are similar to that of any forensic *trace material* such as fibres, paint and glass. Locard's theorem or Locard's exchange principle is the principle of trace evidence transfer. This principle was first enunciated by a French police scientist early last century (Locard, 1920). Sometimes the theory is summarized as 'every contact leaves a trace'. Whether that trace is *detectable* depends on the quantity and quality of the material and analytical methods used in the detection. The *persistence* of the trace on items depends on the activities after the trace was deposited.

DNA transfer, whether through direct contact or through an intermediary item or items, is a consideration for every case. The method of deposition of DNA is less certain when it cannot be related to a visible deposit such as a blood spatter.

Even when it can be related to a body fluid, types of transfer should be considered. Inadvertent transfer of semen led to the 15 months of imprisonment of a young man for rape – when in fact the offence never occurred (Case 2.1; Vincent, 2010). This inquiry could not confirm the exact pathway of the transfer of the semen/DNA and reported that the deposition could have occurred in a variety of ways. The inquiry also stated 'It is possible to speculate about the probability of transference through various mechanisms, but ultimately it is pointless to do so'.

A case from the author's files illustrates the issues that arise when the accused is apprehended at the crime scene.

CASE 3.3   Presence of Accused at Scene; Trace DNA; Direct versus Indirect Transfer

The accused was stationary in a motor vehicle driven by his son when police apprehended him. They searched the car and found plastic bags containing a quantity of powdered illegal drug. The prosecution alleged a DNA profile was obtained from a combined sample from the entire outer surface of four of these plastic bags (out of seven in total). This DNA profile was partial, mixed and consisted of three contributors; it was trace DNA and could not be related to a biological fluid, time or method of deposition.

The prosecution forensic expert stated it was 11 billion times more likely that the mixed DNA profile originated from the accused and two unknown persons than if it originated from three unknown people (using a likelihood ratio and a continuous model system). In the author's opinion there was not only just a partial match of the reference sample to the mixture sample, the DNA profile was suboptimal and low level with a contribution of at least three individuals to the profile. During the hearing, the defence barrister queried the apprehending police officer.

The officer stated that he had searched the person of the accused before seizing the plastic bags and could not remember if he changed gloves in between. He was not wearing appropriate crime scene protection equipment such as overalls. Transfer of DNA was considered a real possibility in this case by the presiding magistrate and the matter was dismissed.

A DNA profile can routinely be obtained from just a few skin cells. A DNA profile was first obtained from a single cell nearly two decades ago (Findley et al., 1997). Importantly, a DNA profile must still be evaluated for its quality.

It is estimated that a human sheds more than 400,000 skin cells each day (Wickenheiser, 2002). Our clothing, our home, our transport, our social contacts may all be sources of these skin cells. Certain articles may be a reservoir of skin cells, holding DNA from many deposits at many times. Bags, coats, hats, gloves and the insoles of shoes may be infrequently cleaned and contain DNA that has accumulated from the regular wearer and other contacts. This DNA may not only be from cells from the surface of the skin but also from other body secretions such as saliva, mucous, nasal secretions and blood.

Locard described the exchange of trace evidence as 'the silent witness'. He thought that every step, every contact, every touch leaves irrefutable evidence that is only diminished by human failure to understand and wholly utilize its value (Locard, 1920; also see Inman and Rudin, 2001, 2002 for principles). All potential traces should be considered, depending on the activity and its information potential.

And so it is with DNA.

Mechanisms of DNA Transfer

DNA may be deposited directly on an item which is called direct or primary transfer. DNA may also be deposited on an item indirectly through an intermediary item(s) (termed secondary, tertiary or higher level transfer), where there has been no physical contact between the original depositor and the final surface on which the DNA profile was located. Direct, or primary, transfer includes contact but also includes activities within the vicinity of an item such as speaking, coughing and sneezing (Meakin and Jamieson, 2013).

Secondary transfer occurs when a material deposited on an item or person is then transferred to another item or person or onto a different place on the same item/person. There has been no physical contact between the original depositor and the final surface on which the material is located. Any biological substance such as blood, semen, hair, saliva and urine can be transferred like this. Different levels of transfer are depicted in Figure 3.1.

The first study on trace DNA transfer showed that DNA can be recovered from objects touched by hands (van Oorschot and Jones, 1997). The finding regarding touched objects has been much discussed due to its investigative potential.

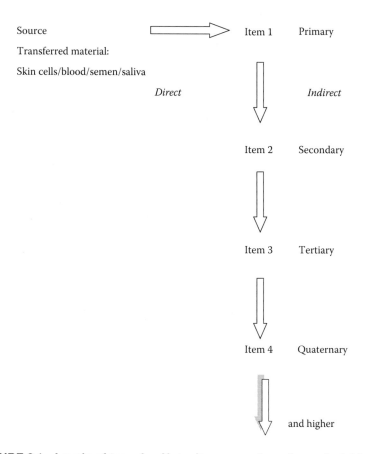

FIGURE 3.1   Levels of transfer. Note: Items may transfer material back to the previous item(s). Primary, secondary and higher refers to the transferred material.

The other findings in this study are just as valuable. Volunteers handling tubes had their hands swabbed, and DNA profiles were observed that matched the previous holders of the tube – the volunteers had not contacted each other. Tubes held for a short time by a second or third person usually provided the DNA profile of the last holder but also provided the DNA of previous holders. The study showed that

- DNA may be transferred from hand to object (direct transfer) and then from object to hand (secondary transfer)
- There may be no physical contact between the original depositor and the final surface on which the DNA profile was located (secondary transfer)

- DNA yields from tubes held for varying lengths of time (5 and 30 seconds; 3 and 10 minutes) did not vary significantly indicating substantial transfer during initial contact
- Hands swabbed before and after a 1 minute handshake revealed the transfer of DNA from one individual to another in one of the four hands tested – thus DNA was not always transferred
- Genetic profiles from objects handled by several people or from minute blood stains on touched objects may be difficult to interpret
- There is a need for caution when handling exhibits and interpreting results

Figure 3.2 shows pathways of hand transfer of DNA.

A biological substance that has been transferred multiple times, if detectable, may appear as components of complex DNA profiles. This is because the *vectors* (such as hands or implements) aiding the transfer, and/or the *substrate* from which it is ultimately collected, may also bear DNA (Goray et al., 2010).

Sometimes the vector may not bear DNA and this could complicate interpretation even further. A study (Fonnelop et al., 2015) found that there could be tertiary transfer when there was no indication of a previous transfer (either direct or indirect; see section 'Higher Levels of Transfer').

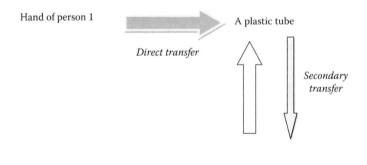

FIGURE 3.2 Pathways of hand transfer. Diagram of handing a plastic tube – consecutive. The hand of person 1 touches the tube and then the hand of person 2 touches the tube. The tube may contain DNA from person 1 plus DNA from person 2. The hand of person 2 may contain DNA from the plastic tube and thus DNA from the hand of person 1.

Another recent study (Cale et al., 2015) on DNA transferred by handling to knives found that secondary DNA transfer was detected in 85% of samples (17 of 20 samples). In five of the samples the secondary contributor was either the only contributor or the major contributor despite never coming into contact with the knife.

An illuminating comment from the above study was that *secondary DNA transfer should not be regarded as an event that may occur under optimal experimental conditions* (this author emphasis).

There is still limited knowledge concerning conditions that may influence secondary or higher transfer. The lack of knowledge regarding the level of transfer in given situations, and of the factors affecting such transfer, makes it difficult to assess the likelihood of alternative case scenarios.

One scientist (Champod, 2013) recently reiterated that there is a need for forensic scientists to highlight how little is known about DNA transfer mechanisms.

An interesting laboratory study from Australia performed experiments that mimicked case scenarios. These were based on prosecution and defence scenarios from adjudicated court cases in Australia and the United States (Goray et al., 2012a). The aim of the study was not to replicate aspects of the case scenarios represented in court, but rather to investigate certain components in a laboratory situation. It presented an insight into the complex nature and behaviour of trace DNA under specific and controlled conditions.

Scenarios involving secondary and tertiary transfer of DNA proposed by the defence in each case were not refuted in these experiments.

CASE 3.4 Direct versus Indirect Transfer; Contamination; Domestic Situation

This was an Australian homicide retrial where the accused had originally been found guilty by a jury in 2004. The case went to appeal, subsequently to the high court, and then to a retrial. This retrial was by judge alone (*Queen v. Hillier*, 2010).

A woman was found strangled and partially burned in her house. The evidence was circumstantial. A tape lift off the lapel of the victim's pyjamas provided a DNA profile that matched the DNA of her ex-partner, who stated he had not been in the house or in contact with her for several months. The DNA was a mixed DNA profile with the major component matching the DNA of the deceased and the minor component matching the DNA of the accused . The ex-partner was charged with murder due to the DNA and other circumstantial evidence.

The case went to appeal and the verdict was overturned. The High Court of Australia then ruled that the possibility of the defendant's DNA on his estranged wife's pyjamas being transferred by their children was not enough reason to overturn a jury's guilty verdict in a murder trial. Rather, a decision should have factored motive and opportunity to kill his wife as well as the unlikelihood of the alternative theory that she was killed by a mystery lover. The case was referred back to a retrial.

The defence had proposed secondary transfer to explain the DNA of the accused on the victim's nightwear. Transfer possibilities presented included from the accused to the children's clothing, or the toys of the children, and then to the nightwear. One forensic expert in the retrial could not exclude the possibility of secondary transfer although another expert thought it was unlikely. The items including clothing from the deceased were opened, unpackaged and examined in a laboratory where officers were bringing in items from the accused (albeit these were packaged). Further tape lifts taken in 2009 from the same area of the nightwear could not replicate the original tape lift DNA result. Contamination or indirect transfer could not be excluded as a reasonable possibility by the presiding judge. The accused was found not guilty.

The laboratory conducting the experiment (Goray et al., 2012a) asked a volunteer to handle toy plastic building blocks by rubbing both hands on all sides of the toy. Five individuals then rubbed all sides of the toy to their laboratory coat (mimicking pyjamas). Each individual was wearing their own laboratory coat which had been worn for 2 days prior. The experiment was repeated with infant singlets placed on dolls.

All but 1 of the 20 coats examined had DNA from the original source observed after contact with the vector (the toy or the singlet). The range of the amount of DNA recovered from the laboratory coats (secondary transfer) was in the same range as the DNA recovered from the toy or singlet (primary transfer). Expected transfer rates were used from previous studies (Goray et al., 2010). Observed transfer rates were generally two to four times greater than the expected.

CASE 3.5 Tertiary Transfer; Work Colleagues with Recent Contact

There was an inquiry by the Australian army into the first military death of an Australian deployed to Iraq (Inquiry, Australian Defence Force, 2006). The man was found shot in the head by his own service pistol in barracks in Baghdad. About an hour prior to his death, he had spent time with a colleague (individual A) at a workstation in the desert, potentially using the same items such as megaphones.

Forensic scientists found DNA matching both individual A and the deceased on the grip and slide of the gun, with individual A being the major contributor. Counsel for individual A said that he did not touch the gun and there could be secondary transfer of DNA from one of the items at the workstation and then further transfer (tertiary) to the gun. A forensic scientist stated that it was unlikely that there was indirect transfer of individual A to the gun considering that there was not a greater amount of DNA from the deceased. They would only have expected secondary transfer from individual A if the deceased had handled his gun within 30 minutes of touching the same objects.

The military inquiry found that the deceased acci-
dentally fired his gun. During 2008 a coronial inquest
returned the same finding.

The laboratory study (Goray et al., 2012a) mimicking this scenario
had a volunteer deposit skin cells on five plastic water hose triggers (representing megaphones). Five other volunteers handled
the hose triggers. They then pursued normal activities for an hour
and then handled plastic guns. Only very partial DNA profiles
were found, and it was considered unlikely for a transfer to generate a full DNA profile under the variables examined. However,
variables such as a hot desert location with perhaps increased
deposition and transfer of DNA through the unusual conditions
could not be replicated.

The third case studied in the laboratory was from the United
States and occurred in 1999. Dr. Dirk Greineder was tried in 2001.

CASE 3.6   Tertiary Transfer; Victim and Accused Cohabiting

A husband and wife both used the same towel to wipe
their faces prior to walking their dog in the park.
While walking, the wife became tired and so she stayed
behind, and her husband continued walking with the
dog. The wife was found strangled and stabbed. Gloves
and a knife were found in a drain at the scene with DNA
matching that of the husband and that of an unknown
person.

The defence postulated that the husband's DNA
was found due to tertiary or further transfer; the husband's DNA was transferred to the towel, then to the
wife's face, and then the gloves and the knife by the
perpetrator. A study was performed by a private forensic laboratory to test the proposition, and they simulated a man and then a woman wiping their face on a
towel, and then gloves and a knife were rubbed against
the woman's face (Taylor, 2004). DNA tests revealed

a mixture of the man and woman on the gloves and knife (tertiary transfer). The jury ultimately convicted the defendant for first-degree murder – there was other circumstantial evidence and he was sentenced to life imprisonment.

The Massachusetts Supreme Court affirmed the judgment, but the U.S. Supreme Court vacated it and remanded the case in light of the recent U.S. Supreme Court decision in Williams v. Illinois. That decision addressed admissibility of DNA evidence, regarding a scientist summarizing the DNA test results performed by another person. The supreme judicial court rejected the appeal (*Commonwealth v. Greineder*, 2013).

The laboratory study (Goray et al., 2012a) obtained blood from a single donor and applied it to a plastic mask (representing the husband's face). A face towel was then applied to the first mask and then wiped over a second plastic mask (representing the wife's face). A volunteer was then asked to 'strangle' the second mask wearing new latex gloves, and then held a kitchen knife.

The results for all transfer steps in this study were greatly different from those expected using the previously generated data of transfer rates. The transfer of DNA to the towel from the second mask (the wife) was higher than expected (54% versus 3%). Unexpectedly, a small proportion of the observed DNA on the gloves appeared to be derived from the wearer of the gloves even though only the outside of the glove was sampled.

The article describing these simulation experiments (Goray et al., 2012a) noted that further research into the issue of DNA transfer is of paramount importance given that forensic practitioners are increasingly required to provide opinions on the likelihoods of different DNA transfer scenarios.

Several factors may influence secondary or higher transfer of DNA. These include the type of biological substance deposited, the nature of the primary and secondary substrate, the moisture content of the deposit and the type of contact between the surfaces. These factors are those typically considered in the transfer of *trace material* in general.

It was recently confirmed (Fonnelop et al., 2015) that the amount of DNA deposited on an object, and the type of substrate on which it is deposited, affects the probability of a transfer.

A review from 2013 (Meakin and Jamieson, 2013) stated that is not currently possible for forensic practitioners to opine on the mechanism of transfer of trace DNA. Specifically, the authors stated that from current scientific data, it is not possible to use the amount or quality of DNA recovered from an item of interest to inform whether the DNA was deposited by direct contact or indirect transfer.

Higher Levels of Transfer

Levels of DNA transfer that were higher than tertiary (derived through at least two intermediary items) were postulated in a study from 2006 (Poy and van Oorschot, 2006a). The extent and origin of DNA material was investigated, and swabs or tape lifts from items on or around an examination bench were taken in an attempt to determine background levels of DNA in the laboratory. Also see section 'Environmental Monitoring and Crime Scene Sampling'.

A magnification lamp in the laboratory yielded an almost full DNA profile and matched a number of samples on a database, related to the one case. It was discovered that one blood stain and one trace sample were taken from the same item, described as a 'bulky jacket', 3 months prior to the swabbing of the magnifying lamp. The study suggested that the DNA appearing on the top side of the lamp was due to the transfer from the jacket on to a glove and then from the glove on to the lamp while examining the jacket. A quaternary and even higher transfer of DNA may have occurred subsequently. This is from jacket to glove (secondary) to lamp (tertiary) to other glove (quaternary) to other exhibit (fifth substrate).

Another finding from the study was that there were items that were considered to pose a low risk for contamination, including floors and taps. This was because multiple transfer steps from an examination would be required to produce a DNA profile. However, only one out of six items did not provide a DNA profile, and the origin of these profiles remained unknown. This finding demonstrates the prevalence of DNA in the laboratory, even on items deemed to be low risk.

One study aimed to measure if a DNA source could be detected after multiple transfer events (Lehmann et al., 2013). Experiments were performed from cotton to cotton, and glass to glass, for wet and dried blood and touch DNA. Transfer from wet blood gave a full DNA profile well beyond secondary transfer on both cotton and glass substrates. In fact, full profiles were obtained from the *sixth* substrate of both wet and dried blood. Touch DNA produced partial DNA profiles up to the *fifth* substrate. A later study found that touch DNA produced full DNA profiles up to the third substrate (Fonnelop et al., 2015).

A very interesting finding from one study demonstrated the quaternary transfer of DNA (Fonnelop et al., 2015). There were unknown fragments of DNA on some of the transfers investigated. These transfers were mediated by a particular individual and the DNA was from the first, second and third substrates. These DNA fragments were later found to match the DNA of the girlfriend of the individual. The girlfriend had not visited the office where the sampling had been performed and had not been in contact with the individual for 10 hours prior. The individual had also washed his hands before the experiments.

Touch

The term 'touch DNA' is reserved in this book for DNA that has proposed to originate through 'touching' or 'handling' and derives predominantly from skin cells.

The hands and fingernails can act as ready vectors for the transmission of disease (in the medical context) or evidence (in the forensic context). Blood or other body fluid or cellular material may transfer from hand to hand in multiple transfer events, and the hands and fingernails may also act as a 'reservoir' of DNA or body material. The hands and fingernails may transfer nasal secretions, saliva, fluid from the eyes/nose/mouth or body fluid from the wounds or orifices of the individual themselves or from other individuals.

The persistence of body fluid or any DNA on the fingernails or hands depends on the activities after the DNA or body fluid was deposited. It will also depend on the location and may remain relatively longer in an area where it is less likely to be dislodged, such as in crevices or underneath the nails.

A review has published a list of amounts of DNA recovered from bare hands or surfaces touched once with bare hands (Meakin and Jamieson, 2013). This amount varies widely, from 0 to 150 ng (nanogram, or a billionth of a gram). One cell contains about 6 pg (picogram, one thousandth of a nanogram) of DNA content. As has been mentioned previously, a DNA profile has been obtained from just one cell (Findlay et al., 1997) although this was from enhanced techniques.

Skin-to-skin contact, such as during physical assaults, has been investigated in the context of manual strangulation. Detectable levels of non-self DNA are normally present on surfaces of necks, especially when they are cohabiting with other individuals. Thus, any DNA obtained from a neck in a strangulation case may, or may not, be from the assailant (Meakin and Jamieson, 2013).

Fingernail Swabs and Cuttings

Fingernail clippings and swabs have been routinely taken for decades during the autopsy of a deceased. They are used as evidence in 'cold cases' because they may be one of few surviving samples from the original investigation.

It is less common to take samples from a suspect unless there is a relatively short time since the event.

The only evidence against the accused in a murder case from the United States comprised DNA from underneath the fingernails of a deceased.

CASE 3.7   Scene-to-Scene Contamination

A millionaire was found dead in his mansion in California in 2012. He had suffocated and been bound and gagged during a home invasion (Kaplan, 2014). The forensic laboratory found foreign DNA underneath the fingernails of the murdered man. The foreign DNA profile was loaded onto the DNA database and matched that of 26-year-old Lukis Anderson, a local homeless man. He was arrested and spent nearly 5 months in prison. He could not recall his whereabouts that night.

But Lukis Anderson had an excellent alibi – at the time of the murder, he was hospitalized and unconscious, with a blood alcohol reading five times the legal limit. The same paramedics that conveyed him to the hospital from outside a liquor store had, some 2 hours later, attended to the murder scene and attempted to revive the deceased. Videotapes and interviews revealed that an oxygen monitoring probe was clipped onto Anderson's finger, and potentially the same probe was also clipped onto the deceased's finger.

The following case is from the author's files and raised the question of transfer of DNA in a social relationship.

CASE 3.8   DNA from Victim to Accused, Recent Casual Contact

The male accused had stated he spent the previous 3 days in an intermittent 'friendly' relationship (no sexual activity) with the female victim and had been in her apartment. The victim had bled from another injury. The accused had not washed and swabs were taken from his person approximately 12 hours after the contact.

There was a quantity of blood and DNA detected from the fingernails of both hands of the accused. It was possible that both the accused and the victim could have contributed to the DNA detected from both hands. It was not possible, however, to determine whether the DNA from each individual, or different body fluids, was deposited at the same or separate times. There was DNA matching the victim on the penile swabs from the accused. The prosecution proposed that there was direct penetration of the vagina of the victim to account for the DNA on the penile swabs; the defence postulated indirect transfer of DNA. The defence argued the inability to determine whether trace DNA was deposited by direct or indirect transfer. The jury did not agree with the proposition of vaginal penetration by the accused, and he was acquitted on this count.

There have been some recent studies published in the forensic science literature on foreign DNA obtained from fingernails (clippings or swabs).

A study from 40 volunteers (Dowlman et al., 2010) showed that good-quality DNA profiles from fingernails were associated with recent intimate contact and were also obtained from individuals who shared accommodation with their partners, flatmates and/or children. Low-level profiles were associated with all levels of contact.

Another study found that variable amounts of foreign DNA can be found in fingernail samples from cohabiting couples without any sexual contact having occurred (Malsom et al., 2009).

The detection of DNA from beneath the fingernails appears as varied as the detection of DNA from any other surface with variables such as time since prior activities, length of time the donor and recipient spend together and method of DNA recovery.

Packaging

Questions regarding how exhibits were packaged, handled and transported were investigated in a study. It found that significant quantities of DNA are frequently (1) transferred from an exhibit to the inside of its packaging and (2) transferred from its area of initial deposit to other areas of the same exhibit and/or to other exhibits within the same package (Goray et al., 2012b). These findings highlight the need to deal with issues inherent in the collection and packaging of exhibits for forensic DNA analysis.

An interesting finding was that cigarette butts packaged together and transported together may transfer DNA to each other. Smoked butts from two different smokers were placed in a package with unsmoked cigarette butts. After transportation, partial DNA profiles of one smoker were found on butts smoked from another person in all cases, and DNA was found on the unsmoked butts in 86% of cases.

Another notable finding was that DNA was lost to the inside of containers holding bloodied knives. There was redistribution of DNA-containing material from the blade of the knife to other areas of the knife, including the handle.

Examination

The occurrence of indirect transfer raises issues regarding the recovery and examination of items from a crime scene. Gloves and tools used in the examination can become contaminated, not only by direct transfer of DNA from the examiner but also by indirect transfer from the exhibits that are being examined.

A study from nearly a decade ago indicated the potential risk of gloves and equipment in examination of exhibits for DNA (Poy and van Oorschot, 2006a). This was discussed in the section 'Touch' with regard to higher-level transfer. Gloved hands could be capable of picking up DNA-containing material from exhibits being examined and transferred to other areas of the exhibit and/or tools while examining. High-risk tools such as scissor blades and tongue forceps are routinely cleaned between exhibit examinations – but their handles, containers, tissue boxes, pipettes and examination lamps that are touched by gloved hands during examination may not.

A study demonstrated that DNA material can be transferred from exhibit to exhibit by scissors, forceps and gloves (Szukata et al., 2015). They pose a significant contamination risk if not DNA-free before contact is made with the targeted sample during exhibit examination. The reuse of instruments and further contact with other areas of an exhibit could potentially relocate DNA, which could negatively affect the interpretation of relevant activities. The potential of intra-exhibit transfer is greater with touch DNA and trace samples as they are less visible – thus increasing the probability of accidental contact during examination.

Gloves, Scissors and Forceps

When searching a crime scene or examining an item, an officer or an analyst may inadvertently transfer DNA from one item to another or to different sites of the same item, even when wearing the appropriate equipment such as gloves (Meakin and Jamieson, 2013). Gloves need to be changed frequently, not only between items but also between different areas of the same item especially when sampling for DNA analysis.

The following case concerned the transfer of DNA (Balding, 2013; Fonnelop et al., 2015; Gill, 2014; Vecchiotti and Zoppis, 2013).

CASE 3.9   Transfer; Contamination; Social Contact between Victim and Accused

The inquiry into the murder of British student Meredith Kercher in Perugia, Italy, has played out in the media. The 21-year-old was found stabbed and sexually assaulted in her bedroom in an apartment she shared with three other female students. One of these, the U.S. citizen Amanda Knox, was charged with the murder together with Raffaele Sollecito, the former Italian boyfriend of Ms. Knox. The Ivory Coast–born Rudy Guede is currently serving a 16-year sentence for the sexual assault and murder; his conviction was apparently uncontroversial. Knox and Sollecito were convicted in 2009, but after spending 4 years in prison, an appellate court in 2011 acquitted them. The acquittal was later overturned.

The key evidence in the case was DNA obtained from a knife found at Sollecito's flat in the kitchen drawer and from bra clasps from the deceased located at the crime scene. The knife allegedly had traces of DNA from Amanda Knox on the handle and of Meredith Kercher on the blade. The DNA alleged to have come from Knox was not disputed (she regularly visited her boyfriend's flat), but the DNA profile alleged to have come from Kercher was low level and could not be related to blood. It was not obvious why the knife was believed to be evidential, and questions were raised about handling and packaging.

The bra clasps were recovered from the scene 46 days after the crime in a context highly suggestive of environmental contamination. It was agreed by all parties that Sollecito may have contributed to the DNA, but the question still remained as to how it was deposited. The defence proposed that an investigator may have inadvertently transferred the DNA from Sollecito on the door handle of the bedroom to the bra clasp.

The Italian Supreme Court in 2015 overturned the convictions of Knox and Sollecito. Chapter 6 further discusses this case.

One study simulated part of the aforementioned scenario by examining the transfer of touch DNA from a metal door handle to a piece of material (Fonnelop et al., 2015). It was found that the simulated tertiary transfer (person to door handle to glove to material) could produce the DNA of the original person on the material.

Another study (Szukata et al., 2015) found that gloves were a highly efficient transfer vector. The flexible nature of a glove surface was considered to be part of the reason for the greater transfer of DNA via gloves than scissors or forceps. A further reason could be the greater surface area of the glove.

Implements such as scissors and forceps tend to have non-flexible surfaces, unlike gloves. There is also less surface area contact when examining the exhibit. Scissor blades and forcep tips are smaller in size than gloves.

The study (Szukata et al., 2015) recommended the following:

- Using disposable forceps and scissors
- Cleaning of gloves with the appropriate agent before use
- Changing of gloves each time after touching the surface of an exhibit
- Wearing multiple gloves to reduce skin exposure when changing gloves
- Reducing handling of items if later sampling for DNA

Fingerprinting

It was described in 2005 that fingerprint brushes could potentially collect and transfer DNA and the same brush could powder different items of evidence within and between crime scenes (van Oorschot et al., 2005). The dusting of latent prints may dislodge cellular debris and that debris may adhere to the brush. This brush can then potentially be used on another item where it also may transfer dislodged cellular debris.

A more recent study (Bolivar et al., 2015) found that detection of secondary transfer can occur through fingerprint brush contamination and is enhanced using low template DNA methods (see Chapter 6 for these methods).

Mortuary

Samples taken during an autopsy are often submitted for DNA analysis. An investigation (Rutty et al., 2000) of 20 mortuaries in the United Kingdom was launched in the late 1990s when two instances of contamination were reported. Of those mortuaries investigated, at least half had quantifiable human DNA on instruments and mortuary surfaces. Mortuary scissors were the most frequently contaminated instrument – with profiles from one to three individuals obtained.

A later study from Germany found that DNA could be obtained from most samples from instruments and autopsy tables and could be linked to bodies that had been autopsied previously (Schwark et al., 2012). The study showed that in four of the six cases investigated, DNA from a previously autopsied body had been transferred via the autopsy table to the present body. The higher incidence of contamination in this study compared to the UK study was thought to be a result of the increased sensitivity of DNA profiling techniques in the intervening decade.

The mortuary may provide vast quantities of DNA due to the expulsion of body fluids during the autopsy. While the autopsy may not involve the search for trace evidence as in a forensic examination, the transfer of material (whether trace or larger) from previous autopsies requires recognition and mitigation.

Environmental Monitoring and Crime Scene Sampling

Any background DNA on surfaces and equipment in a laboratory examination pose a contamination risk (Poy et al., 2006b). Forensic laboratories have implemented DNA environmental monitoring programs to identify and monitor risk for contamination.

It is unknown whether crime scene examination offices have these types of programs. If an item is scraped, swabbed or tape lifted to obtain a sample for DNA, then it is also necessary to ensure extraneous DNA is not introduced from surfaces or implements.

More sensitive typing kits may require a reassessment of environmental and cleaning programs. It was shown that a move from a 10-marker Profiler Plus system to a 21-marker PowerPlex21 system resulted in DNA obtained from items that had been previously DNA-free (Ballantyne et al., 2013). Approximately 70% of the environmental samples displayed a positive amplification result with PowerPlex21 compared with 23% of the samples with Profiler Plus.

The presence of background DNA on laboratory surfaces, together with the principle of 'control' sections of an exhibit, leads to the idea of sampling additional areas of the crime scene for 'background' DNA. For example if a piece of fabric is on a table at a crime scene, then sampling/swabbing areas adjacent to the fabric may be beneficial.

DNA 'Dust'

It is believed that, in addition to contact, DNA may transfer by aerosols (Fonnelop et al., 2015). Human cells already present in the surrounds, such as house dust, may be transferred to exhibits through their presence in the 'air'. Terms such as DNA 'falling from the ceiling' have been used (author information).

Inadvertent Transfer and Contamination

The modes of transfer of DNA are varied, as described in this chapter. Direct and indirect transfer needs to be considered in the interpretation of a DNA profile.

Contamination of an item with DNA implies the accidental transfer of DNA. The DNA has not been transferred during the crime event. This contaminating DNA may be deposited during collection, during preservation or handling or during the analysis – or all three.

Contamination and its prevention is part of quality control and is further discussed in Chapter 9.

The investigator-mediated transfer of trace DNA may not necessarily reveal mixtures involving the investigator if investigators wear suitable protective clothing. The transfer of DNA from a glove to an exhibit, if that glove had previously touched another item, is a tertiary transfer and may not be realized as such because *the glove is not sampled for DNA.*

The 'hidden perpetrator effect' has been recently proposed (Gill, 2014). It is not inevitable that DNA will be recovered from the offender at a crime scene. If the perpetrator DNA is missing at the scene, then donors of background and investigator-mediated contaminant trace DNA will automatically become suspects. An investigator may believe that a DNA profile recovered from a crime scene must have something to do with the crime. Consequently, the true perpetrator may be 'hidden'.

This chapter has described that DNA may, or may not, be detectable when surfaces contact each other. It may not persist on an item. A DNA profile alone cannot inform when or how the DNA was deposited. The amount of DNA also cannot inform whether the DNA was transferred directly, or indirectly.

Nevertheless, the forensic scientist must still consider and present to the courts the various ways that DNA can transfer, in the context of the case, and using the scientific method. The assumptions and limitations of the tests can then be conveyed.

References

Australian Defence Force. 2006. Transcript of proceedings: Inquiry into the death of PTE Jacob Bruce Kovco. National Transcription Service: Melbourne, Australia. Available at: http://www.defence.gov.au/publications/kovcoreport.pdf, accessed 24 November 2015.

Balding, D. 2013. Evaluation of mixed source low template DNA profiles in forensic science. *Proc. Natl. Acad. Sci. USA* 110(30): 12241–12246.

Ballantyne, K., Poy, A.L. and van Oorschot, R.A. 2013. Environmental DNA monitoring: Beware of the transition to more sensitive methodologies. *Aust. J. Forensic Sci.* 45(3): 323–340.

Bolivar, P.-A., Tracey, M. and McCord, B. 2015. Assessing the risk of secondary transfer via fingerprint brush contamination using enhanced sensitivity DNA analysis methods. *J. Forensic Sci.* First published online 24 August 2015.

Cale, C.M., Earll, M.L., Latham, K.E. and Bush, G.L. 2015. Could secondary DNA transfer falsely place someone at the scene of a crime? *J. Forensic Sci.* 1–8. First published online 1 September 2015.

Champod, C. 2013. DNA transfer: Informed judgment or mere guesswork? *Front. Genet.* 4: 300.

Commonwealth v. Dirk K. Greineder. 2013. Massachusetts Supreme Court. SJC-08866a USA.

Dowlman, E.A., Martin, N.C., Foy, M.J. et al. 2010. The prevalence of mixed DNA profiles in fingernail swabs. *Sci. Justice* 50(2): 64–71.

Findley, I., Taylor, A., Quirke, P. et al. 1997. DNA fingerprinting from single cells. *Nature* 389: 555–556.

Fitzgerald v. The Queen. 2014. High Court of Australia. HCA 28 and HCA Trans 048.

Fonnelop, A.E., Egeland, T. and Gill, P. 2015. Secondary and subsequent DNA transfer during criminal investigation. *Forensic Sci. Int. Genet.* 17: 155–162.

French, J. and Morgan, R. 2015. An experimental investigation of the indirect transfer and deposition of gunshot residue: Further studies carried out with SEM-EDX analysis. *Forensic Sci. Int.* 247: 14–17.

Gill, P. 2014. *Misleading DNA Evidence: Reasons for Miscarriage of Justice.* Academic Press: London, U.K.

Goray, M., Eken, E., Mitchell, J. et al. 2010. Secondary DNA transfer of biological substances under varying test conditions. *Forensic Sci. Int. Genet.* 4: 62–67.

Goray, M., Mitchell, J. and van Oorschot, R.A. 2012a. Evaluation of multiple transfer of DNA using mock case scenarios. *J. Legal Med.* 14(1): 40–46.

Goray, M., van Oorschot, R.A. and Mitchell, J. 2012b. DNA transfer within forensic exhibit packaging: Potential for DNA loss and relocation. *Forensic Sci. Int. Genet.* 6: 158–166.

Inman, K. and Rudin, N. 2001. *Principles and Practice of Criminalistics: The Profession of Forensic Science.* CRC Press: Boca Raton, FL.

Inman, K. and Rudin, N. 2002. The origin of evidence. *Forensic Sci. Int.* 126: 11–16.

Kaplan, T. 2014. Monte Sereno murder case casts doubt on DNA evidence. *San Jose Mercury News*, 28 June 2014.

Lehmann, V.J., Mitchell, R.J., Ballantyne, K.N. et al. 2013. Following the transfer of DNA: How far can it go? *Forensic Sci. Int. Genet. Suppl.* 4: e53–e54.

Locard, E. 1920. *L'enquête criminelle et les méthodes scientifiques.* Flammarion: Paris, France.

Malsom, S., Flanagan, N., McAlister, C. and Dixon, L. 2009. The prevalence of mixed DNA profiles in fingernail samples taken from couples who co-habit using autosomal and Y-STRs. *Forensic Sci. Int. Genet.* 3: 57–62.

Meakin, G. and Jamieson, A. 2013. DNA transfer: Review and implications for casework. *Forensic Sci. Int. Genet.* 7: 434–443.

Poy, A. and van Oorschot, R.A. 2006a. Beware; gloves and equipment used during the examination of exhibits are potential vectors for transfer of DNA-containing material. *Int. Congr. Ser.* 1288: 556–558.

Poy, A. and van Oorschot, R.A. 2006b. Trace DNA presence, origin, and transfer within a forensic biology laboratory and its potential effect on casework. *J. Forensic Ident.* 56: 558–576.

Queen v. Hillier. 2010. Supreme Court of the Australian Capital Territory. ACTSC 33.

Queen v. Sumner and Fitzgerald. 2013. 117 SASR 271 Australia.

Rutty, G.N., Watson, S. and Davison, J. 2000. DNA contamination of mortuary instruments and work surfaces: A significant problem in forensic practice? *Int. J. Legal Med.* 114: 56–60.

Schwark, T., Poetsch, M., Preusse-Prange, A. et al. 2012. Phantoms in the mortuary – DNA transfer during autopsies. *Forensic Sci. Int.* 216(1): 121–126.

Szukata, B., Harvey, M., Ballantyne, K.N. et al. 2015. DNA transfer by examination tools – A risk for forensic casework? *Forensic Sci. Int. Genet.* 16: 246–254.

Taupin, J.M. 1996. Hair and fiber transfer in an abduction case – Evidence from different levels of trace evidence transfer. *J. Forensic Sci.* 41(4): 697–699.

Taupin, J.M. and Cwiklik, C. 2010. *Scientific Protocols for Forensic Examination of Clothing.* CRC Press: Boca Raton, FL.

Taylor, M. 2004. Study of DNA transfer. Available at: http://www.biofo rensics.com/conference04/Transfer/Taylor&Johnson%20Study.pdf, accessed 24 November 2015.

Van Oorschot, R.A. and Jones, M. 1997. DNA fingerprints from fingerprints. *Nature* 387: 767.

Van Oorschot, R.A, Treadwell, S., Beaurepaire, J. et al. 2005. *J. Forensic Sci.* 50(6): 1417–1421.

Vecchiotti, C. and Zoppis, S. 2013. DNA and the law in Italy: The experience of "the Perugia case". *Front. Genet.* 4: 177.

Vincent, H.F. 2010. Inquiry into the circumstances that led to the conviction of Mr. Farah Abdulkadir Jama. Victorian Government Printer: Melbourne, Victoria, Australia.

Wickenheiser, R. 2002. Trace DNA: A review, discussion of theory and the application of the transfer of trace quantities of DNA through skin contact. *J. Forensic Sci.* 47(3): 442–450.

Chapter **4**

Interpretation of DNA Profiles

Introduction

'DNA' stands for 'deoxyribonucleic acid'. It is a molecule that holds the information and instructions for an organism. There are 23 chromosomes, bundles of genes, in the human 'genome' of the molecule. Half our DNA is inherited from our mother (from the egg in fertilization) and half from our father (from the spermatozoa).

Each person's DNA remains the same over their life and has the same composition throughout the body. This is exploited in DNA profiling as the DNA from a blood/semen/skin cell deposit at a *crime* scene can be compared with the DNA from a *reference* mouth (cell) swab from a victim or suspect.

Parts of DNA are 'tandemly repeated' sequences, and the variations between these tandem repeats in humans are called polymorphisms. Short tandem repeats (STRs) are used in forensic science and tend to be tetra (4) repeats which are repeated 5–30 times. Markers, which examine different locations on the molecule, are typically chosen from separate chromosomes to avoid any problems with linkage between the markers (see Chapter 5).

A genotype is the set of alleles in a human; an allele is an alternative form of a gene. A 'homozygous' genotype means that there are two identical alleles at the same locus (plural loci); the same allele number has been inherited from both the mother and the father, for example a 16,16. A 'heterozygous' genotype means that there are two different alleles at the same locus; different alleles were inherited from the mother and the father, for example '16,18'.

A DNA profile is the combination of genotypes obtained for different loci. It is important to remember that multiple loci are examined in DNA profiling to reduce the possibility of a coincidental match between unrelated individuals.

Human beings have cells that contain the DNA. The size of an animal cell is about 10–20 micrometres (μm) which is about a fifth of the size that may be visible to the naked eye.

A plant cell is about 100 μm in diameter, an animal cell about 10 μm, to 1 μm for bacteria and 0.1 μm for a virus. Finally, an atom has a diameter of about 1 Å or ten thousandth of a micrometre (Alberts et al., 2002). Figure 4.1 depicts the relative sizes of cells.

Human and animal cells are not only tiny but also colourless and translucent. Staining techniques are used to visualize the cells

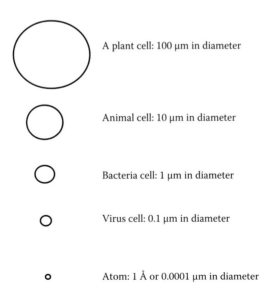

A plant cell: 100 μm in diameter

Animal cell: 10 μm in diameter

Bacteria cell: 1 μm in diameter

Virus cell: 0.1 μm in diameter

Atom: 1 Å or 0.0001 μm in diameter

FIGURE 4.1 Relative sizes of cells (not to scale).

under a microscope with magnification. Sperm and skin cells are quite different in appearance. Sperm appear like tadpoles (with or without the tails) and skin cells are round to oval.

The DNA obtained in a forensic investigation needs to be in a form that can be interpreted and compared to DNA obtained from other people. Obtaining DNA from *inside* the 'nucleus' (core) of the cells is the mainstream form of DNA profiling. A type of analysis that focuses on the Y chromosome, a sex-determining gene from inside the nucleus, is called Y-STR profiling. This type of DNA profiling is discussed in Chapter 7.

Mitochondrial DNA is found in the mitochondria *outside* the nucleus of the cell but still within the cell membrane. Different techniques are used to locate and analyze this mitochondrial DNA. This type of DNA profiling is used in the analysis of human and animal DNA (see Chapter 7).

DNA profiling is used as a *comparative* technique. The DNA result of a crime sample is compared with that obtained from a reference sample from a person. DNA profiles are relatively straight forward to interpret when there is sufficient DNA, and it appears to be from a single source. Mixtures and partial profiles of DNA introduce further complexity. The resulting potential lower discrimination and evidential value could be crucial in a criminal case, and these issues are further discussed in Chapters 5 and 6.

The particular technical steps in the process to produce a DNA profile are explained in detail in forensic DNA texts such as Butler (2012).

The main steps in the technical process for DNA profiling are as follows:

- Sample the crime deposit and separate biological matter if possible.
- Extract the DNA and clean up the sample.
- Measure the quantity of the DNA.
- Target the specific areas of interest within the DNA molecule and the repeat fragments.
- Produce multiple copies of these fragments.
- Sort the fragments according to size and measure against a standard.

A major advantage of STR profiling is that many areas on the DNA molecule can be examined simultaneously, in systems called 'multiplexes', thus reducing the amount of time required for a result.

Sampling: The First Step

The aim of the first steps (indeed all of the steps) in the analytical process is to produce a sufficient quantity and quality of DNA profile. If at all possible, mixtures of biological fluid are avoided in the sampling process. Furthermore, as much DNA from a particular sample is attempted to be obtained in the sampling, extraction, amplification and detection steps. Figure 4.2 illustrates the steps to obtain a DNA profile.

Sometimes, just a swab or a tape lift or a tiny piece of fabric is submitted for examination by other laboratory personnel or from the crime scene. As described in the previous chapters, these samples are removed (in more ways than one) from the initial exhibit, and the context may be lost.

Reference samples from suspects, victims and other relevant people are usually analyzed at separate locations in the laboratory (sometimes in different cities) to the crime samples. This is to mitigate any cross-transfer, but sometimes this is not so.

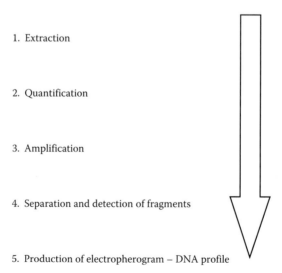

1. Extraction

2. Quantification

3. Amplification

4. Separation and detection of fragments

5. Production of electropherogram – DNA profile

FIGURE 4.2   Steps in obtaining a DNA profile from a biological sample.

The following case from the United States describes an example of incorrect placing of samples in vials, and a DNA database match that subsequently excluded the original accused (Innocence Project).

CASE 4.1 Sample Switch; Database Exclusion

A masked man in a blue hooded sweatshirt and ski mask burst into a woman's home in Las Vegas in 2001 and forced her to drive to an ATM for money. He ran away when the woman's husband spotted them. Police followed 18-year-old Dwayne Jackson and his cousin Howard Grissom who were riding bikes and thought they could be the suspects. They looked inside a car in the driveway of their house and discovered a blue hooded sweatshirt with a ski mask in the pocket. Both Jackson and Grissom denied involvement.

Jackson's DNA profile matched that from the DNA on the sweatshirt. The DNA was the only evidence connecting him to the crime. Jackson pleaded guilty as the other charges of kidnapping and burglary carrying lengthy terms would be dropped if he did. He was imprisoned for 4 years and released in 2006.

During November 2010, the California authorities contacted Las Vegas police and informed them that someone else in the DNA database system matched the crime scene sample for the crime for which Jackson had been convicted. Howard Grissom had been sentenced for an unrelated kidnapping and attempted murder in southern California in 2008, and he was serving a 41-year jail term. It was his DNA profile that matched the DNA profile from the sweatshirt. It was discovered through a forensic review and reanalysis that a laboratory technician had put Johnson's sample into Grissom's reference vial and vice versa in the original case.

Dwayne Jackson was pardoned in 2011.

We can predict that DNA profiles produced from references will be single source and good quality. If they are not, then a further sample from the person can be taken. Crime stains are not so amenable.

The association of a particular body fluid and a DNA profile is not implicit (Peel and Gill, 2004; Taupin and Cwiklik, 2010). It would be desirable if DNA from different types of body material could be differentiated. Currently, however, DNA profiling does not reveal what body fluid or tissue source from which the DNA profile originated.

The only cells that can be separated are sperm (the 'male seed') from other cells. Skin cells from different people, or within one person's body, cannot be separated.

Extraction

Extraction of the DNA from the sample is the next step. The cell membrane is broken open to release the DNA. The process also aims to remove protein and other matter so that inhibition from these materials in the copying process (see amplification step) is reduced.

The method of extraction of the DNA from the sample will depend on the nature of the sample. Epithelial cells from 'touch' DNA require a simpler and quicker extraction to isolate the DNA than that from spermatozoa or hair roots.

Samples from crime scenes require scientific judgement as to the method of extraction. Dyes from within the substrate such as denim jeans may colour the extract, with consequent inhibition of the amplification. Additional material may degrade the DNA itself, such as mould.

The resulting DNA profile obtained may reflect inhibition or degradation of the sample. Another extraction technique, and a repeat DNA analysis, may be required on the sample to obtain an optimum profile. Evidence of degradation or inhibition of the DNA in the sample may be observed in the DNA profile itself (see the following text).

When DNA profiling was first introduced in 1986, a method of separation of sperm from cells was also introduced (Case 1.1; Gill and Werrett, 1987). 'Differential lysis' selectively enriches the sperm concentration in vaginal fluid/semen mixtures, thereby avoiding the problem of the victim's DNA (which is in great excess) masking the male perpetrator. This is the only protocol to have remained unchanged throughout the past three decades in forensic laboratories.

The following case study shows how contamination occurred between two separate cases in the DNA extraction step of the analysis (Rennison, 2012).

CASE 4.2   Extraction Contamination; Database Match

A young man from the south of England was accused of raping a woman in Manchester, a city in the north to which he claimed he had never been. Adam Scott subsequently spent 5 months on remand in custody after it was allegedly found, through a database search, that his DNA profile matched that of the semen found on a medical sample from the woman. The DNA was the sole evidence against the accused. He was released in March 2012 after being found 'the innocent victim of an avoidable contamination'.

The two low vaginal swabs, two high vaginal swabs and two vulval swabs from the woman were found to have semen. This semen was separated from the cellular material (the differential lysis or extraction process) to remove the female cells. All the swabs had male DNA profiles from the semen fraction that were identified as the victim's boyfriend. One of the vulval swabs produced a mixed profile containing the victim's boyfriend and another incomplete DNA profile. The unknown male DNA profile was loaded onto the national DNA database. There was a partial DNA profile match of Scott with a probability of 'one in one billion' of obtaining chance DNA components in an unrelated person. The opinion of the scientist was that the DNA matching Scott most likely came from the semen.

The government inquiry found that a plastic tray sample holder was mistakenly reused and loaded into equipment by a laboratory worker as part of the robotic DNA extraction process, instead of being disposed into a rubbish bin. Saliva from Scott from an unconnected earlier 'spitting incident' was extracted in the same tray 'well' before the DNA from the vulval swab from the woman. Basic procedures for the disposal of plastic trays were not followed, records not maintained and nothing was done to mark trays once they had been used.

This case had a similar problem to Case 2.1. That is, all the other evidence belied the DNA result. The DNA result was used to prove that the accused had sexual activity with the complainant.

The following are noted:

- Only one of six swabs had DNA that 'matched' the accused.
- DNA from sperm cannot be differentiated from DNA from saliva once extracted.
- It is not possible to imply sexual activity without a consideration of context.
- Remnants of DNA may remain after an extraction, sufficient to produce a searchable profile, and is often thrown away.

A laboratory may state that a sample was processed at different times and by different people, and thus contamination between samples is unlikely. However, this case demonstrates that this may not always be true in the robotic and mass extractions of samples.

Consideration of the time of deposition of semen was important in the following case from the author's files.

CASE 4.3   Time of Deposition; Mixture of Semen; DNA 'Match'; Cold Case

A cold case murder was reopened. The body of a woman was found naked and brutally battered near a walking trail in a national park. A blood-stained rock was near her body which was alleged to have caused her death. Semen was found from medical swabs inside the body. Advances in technology led to DNA obtained from the swabs and then a search of databases.

Two men were charged with the murder. One man pleaded guilty to murder and to unlawful sexual intercourse. The other man said he had consensual sex with the woman before the murder. He claimed he had nothing to do with her murder or of taking her to the park. The defence argued that the evidence was incapable of convincing a jury of his guilt.

There was DNA from the semen of the medical swabs that indicated at least three individuals, and possibly four. The two convicted men were considered to have contributed DNA. There was an 'unknown individual A', never located, who was also considered to have contributed DNA to the mixture.

The judge directed the jury to find the accused not guilty. Even if the DNA matched the accused and showed he had sex with her, it did not prove he participated in the rape and murder of the victim or that he was even present when the crime occurred.

Mixtures of DNA in semen are problematic. If there are two or more male contributors suspected in a sample, then Y-STR may be useful.

Extraction techniques (not just automation) can be adapted and improved if there is a problem suspected in the fabric or substrate on which the biological deposit lays. An intriguing multiple murder from Japan illustrates the principle (Honda, 2015).

CASE 4.4   Extraction; Blood Stains; Degradation

A large fire started about midnight in the office and home of the director of a family-run miso (fermented soy bean paste) factory in 1966. Four corpses were discovered in the burnt out ruins. The bodies had many stab wounds and were identified as the director of the factory, his wife and two of his children. Two months later, an employee of the factory was arrested based on circumstantial evidence, and he confessed after prolonged interrogation (20 days). The prosecution declared that the accused had worn pyjamas during the crime but no blood was found on them. During the trial, some 14 months later, five items of clothing were found in a miso barrel in the factory. The clothing had blood stains in a drip pattern. This clothing was then declared as the clothing worn by the accused and not the pyjamas. There was an ABO blood group B stain on the right shoulder that matched the blood group of the accused. The death sentence was confirmed in 1980 based on this evidence, but a retrial was requested by the defence.

Eventually in 2011 DNA analysis was conducted on the samples from the clothing. Because the samples were contaminated with miso, an extraction method was used to separate the blood from the miso. DNA profiles were able to be obtained. The blood stain samples, which were thought to originate from the victims, could not be interpreted because there were no victim reference samples.

After the DNA results were submitted to the court, a reference sample was obtained from the incarcerated man. His DNA profile did not match the critical DNA profile obtained from the right shoulder of the clothing. A retrial judgment was issued by the court in 2014 recognizing the DNA evidence. The court suspected the items of clothing used in the original trial were forged and the accused man was released immediately.

The day after the accused was released, the managing director's eldest daughter, who had given testimony, was found dead from causes unknown.

Quantification

The main aim of the quantification step is to determine how much of the sample can be added for the amplification stage. The DNA extracted from a crime sample may not just be human but also be, or include, animal and plant DNA. Quantification is human specific (or at least higher primate). STR primers are also human specific.

Ideally all samples will have the same amount of DNA added to the amplification mixture. Too much DNA will result in off-scale peaks, peak imbalance and split peaks. Too little DNA may result in poor-quality profiles. Profiling kits have recommended ranges of the amount of DNA that should be added, which varies from 0.5 to 2.0 nanogram (ng).

If no DNA is quantified, many laboratories previously stopped at this point. Now, many laboratories will go ahead and perform the steps below in order to attempt a DNA profile. The quantification step is known to be less sensitive than the actual profiling step so an attempt at a result may be made if the evidence is considered crucial and/or necessary to the case, even if no DNA is quantified in this step. The absence of a quantifiable amount of DNA in the sample may mean that low-level DNA considerations need to be implemented in any further step in the analysis and interpretation (see Chapter 6).

Amplification

The amount of DNA extracted from forensic samples is very small. Amplification makes many copies of the DNA material. More than a million copies of the target DNA can be obtained in a few hours through a number of amplification 'cycles'.

The technique for the amplification of the extract is called polymerase chain reaction and can be utilized on very small and degraded samples. It targets the 'STRs' with specific sequence 'primers' and these are what are amplified. Each primer is labelled with a fluorescent light-reactive coloured dye in order for detection under a laser in the detection step. Thus the amplification step also enables detection.

A 'cycle' traditionally numbers 28. A higher number of cycles were used to obtain a result from smaller amounts, and increased cycles were used in 'low copy number' techniques (up to 34 cycles). It was stated that a laboratory may not be explicit that low-level techniques are being used (Caddy et al., 2008). The PowerPlex21 kit, using 21 markers on the molecule, uses *30 cycles* in its conventional typing.

Separation and Interpretation

The amplified DNA fragments are separated, detected and analyzed. This is called 'autosomal' STR profiling. There are 22 pairs of 'autosome' chromosomes in humans that are not involved in determining the sex. The remaining pair of chromosomes is the sex-determining X and Y chromosomes.

The detection of dye-labelled fragments is now by capillary electrophoresis. Electrical current is applied to move the samples along the capillary and they are separated. A laser excites the dye labels, and the emission is captured in digital form and ultimately measured (in relative fluorescence units).

A DNA profile is pictured in laboratory case files as an 'electropherogram' (known as 'EPG'), an electronic printout representing the distribution of peaks across the chosen markers. It is this diagram from which scientists determine factors such as the quality and quantity of the DNA present, the number of contributors and artefacts. Figure 4.3 is an example.

The height of the peak is measured in terms of relative fluorescent units (along the vertical axis). The horizontal axis relates to the molecular weight (how large the fragment).

One of the presumptions in determining a 'match' between a crime DNA profile and a reference DNA profile is that the peaks (or alleles) are designated correctly in both profiles. There are three kinds of alleles in a crime stain profile (Gill et al., 2006):

- Alleles which are unmistakeable
- Alleles that may be masked by an artefact
- Alleles that have dropped out completely and are therefore not detected

A forensic DNA report may include a 'table of alleles' which compares the crime scene sample DNA profiles with reference

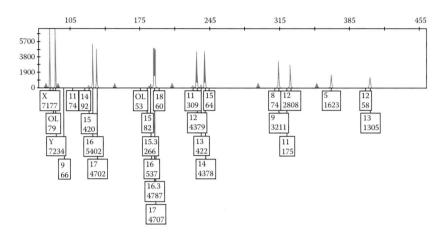

FIGURE 4.3 An electropherogram, diagram of a DNA profile. Representation of DNA fragments; alleles are higher peaks. Vertical axis represents the intensity of signal, correlated to the amount (units in relative fluorescence). Horizontal axis represents the weight of fragment, larger weights to the right of the axis. There are small peaks marked OL, and other small peaks not marked but considered stutter (echo of large peaks).

samples DNA profiles. These tables most often also include the accused sample and the complainant sample. The alleles are those which are designated by the forensic scientist at a particular locus and correspond to the values detected at the locus for a particular profiling system. The PowerPlex21 system examines 21 loci, including amelogenin, the sex marker. Table 4.1 shows a table of alleles of three samples – the crime scene sample, one accused reference sample and one complainant reference sample.

Analytical Threshold

There are thresholds used in the interpretation of a DNA profile and the designation of peaks. The 'analytical' threshold is a level above which a peak may be determined as a real peak, distinguishable from noise. Validation studies should be performed in the particular laboratory to determine the analytical threshold. Some laboratories determine the analytical threshold for each DNA profile or EPG determined on the signal-to-noise ratio.

The stochastic threshold is the other threshold sometimes used in the interpretation of an EPG, particularly with low-level profiles

TABLE 4.1 Table of Alleles as May Be Shown in a Forensic DNA Report

Locus	D3	vWA	D16	D2	AMEL	D8	D21	D18	D19	THO1	FGA
Crime stain	15,16	14,16	9,10	20,23	X,Y	12,15	28,31	12,15	14,15	7,9.3	24,26
Complainant reference	15,16	16,16	10,11	19,22	X,Y	11,12	29,29	12,15	14,14	7,9.3	23,25
Accused reference	15,16	14,16	9,10	20,23	X,Y	12,15	28,31	12,15	14,15	7,9.3	24,26

Notes:

The names of each locus are along the top row in their usual abbreviated form (11 loci, D3 to FGA).

The alleles of the crime stain are represented in the second row under 'crime stain'.

The alleles are numbers under each locus, except for the sex-determining marker amelogenin (AMEL). All profiles are proposed to be from a male and from a single contributor.

The crime stain profile is of 'good quality'.

The accused is included as a contributor to the crime stain from this table. The complainant is excluded as a
contributor.

(discussed further in Chapter 6). Peaks below this threshold may have 'dropout' of their sister allele in a heterozygote.

Sex Marker Amelogenin

One of the loci analyzed on the DNA molecule is called amelogenin which is used for typing the sex of the contributor. Males have X and Y chromosomes and will appear as 'X,Y' in the allele table, or there will be peaks corresponding to the X and Y allele. Females only have the X chromosome and will appear as 'X,X' in the allele table.

The amelogenin locus encodes for a protein in tooth enamel. Reference profiles can be checked to determine if there is any failure of an allele to amplify (mutations).

The sex marker is not used in any statistical evaluation.

If there is a Y allele present, this indicates that there is a male contributor to the DNA. Conversely, if no Y allele is present, this raises the question as to why one would consider a male contribution. The forensic science literature does not discuss whether the Y allele can 'drop out', that is not appear because it is too low in quantity. Figure 4.4 is an EPG, a DNA profile of a mixture of male and female DNA.

Autosomal Markers

Autosomal DNA is that which is inherited from the numbered chromosome pairs, which are from 1 to 22. This excludes the remaining pair of sex chromosomes. The autosomal chromosomes are numbered according to size; for example chromosome 1 has the largest amount of genes and chromosome 22 the smallest.

The autosomal markers in an STR typing kit are those that show the variable number of tandem repeats which are useful in discrimination. The autosomal STRs are involved in the statistical weighting of the DNA.

Artefacts and Other Technical Issues

Artefacts are peaks or other abnormalities in the DNA profile, or EPG. Technical artefacts have been documented extensively and are often observed. Laboratories are required as part of their

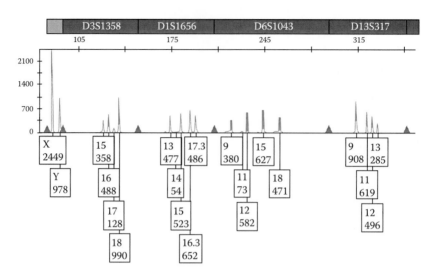

FIGURE 4.4 Electropherogram of mixture of male and female DNA (at 5 loci) from a semen stain. Disparity in heights of X and Y peaks: the female victim is X,X and the male suspect is X,Y. Both male and female individuals are proposed to contribute. At D3, a homozygote contributor of 18,18 is proposed (only 3 peaks considered alleles). Peaks are designated in this profile that correspond to stutter, for example 14 at DIS.

quality system to use protocols to distinguish between artefacts and real DNA peaks. The presence of numerous dye blobs, spikes in the EPG, split peaks and shoulders on peaks may indicate a poor-quality profile that may be a result of poor or sloppy analysis.

Stutter

Artefacts such as *stutter* are very often observed, also in reference DNA profiles. Stutter peaks are artefacts that may arise from imperfect DNA copying during the amplification process. They result from a slippage of the strand during the amplification process and are one repeat unit smaller than the designated allele on the EPG. Occasionally, there will be a 'forward' stutter peak which is four base pairs greater than its associated allele.

Stutter peaks were traditionally evaluated by examining the ratio of the stutter peak height to that of the appropriate adjacent allele, expressed as a percentage (generally not more than 15%). If a peak height was, for example 50% of the parent adjacent peak, then it must be considered that it may have come from another

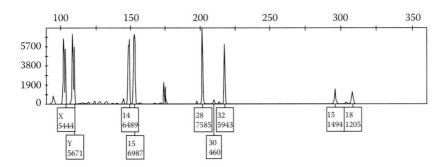

FIGURE 4.5   A DNA profile showing artefacts. Split peaks at amelogenin marker X and Y. Smaller peaks not marked could be stutter, pull up or material from the instrument. Stutter from the 14 allele at second locus.

contributor (mixture). This is obvious in a reference sample, but may not be so in crime samples.

Figure 4.5 is an example of a DNA profile with many artefacts, including stutter.

Mixtures and Number of Contributors

A sample that contains DNA from two or more individuals is referred to as a *mixture*. A single person is expected to contribute at most two alleles for each locus. If more than two peaks are visible at any locus, a mixture should be considered.

When profiles contain DNA from two or more people, the assignment of each allele to a particular individual becomes more difficult. Alleles from one contributor may 'mask' alleles from another contributor.

Degraded, inhibited, limited or poor-quality DNA introduces further complications to the analysis of a DNA profile. This may complicate or confound the analysis. There could be DNA from one or more major contributors with small amounts of DNA from minor contributors.

The minimum number of contributors is usually based on the marker on the DNA molecule (locus) that exhibits the greatest number of allelic peaks (SWGDAM, 2010). However, the number of contributors is often unclear. When a sample is typed in a 10-marker system and then a 21-marker system, it has been recognized that more contributors may be typed in the later system (Ballantyne et al., 2013).

If there is difficulty in determining the number of contributors, then this exacerbates the problem with trying to estimate the DNA profile of any individual who may have contributed to that mixture.

Assumptions in the number of contributors are made by the scientist in order to interpret a DNA profile in some statistical systems. It is not known and can never be known for most casework profiles. It is only known for reference samples.

Stutters and Number of Contributors

Stutter is most problematic when there are multiple contributors to the crime scene DNA profile (Balding and Buckleton, 2009). An allelic peak from a minor contributor can be indistinguishable from a stutter peak generated from a major contributor (Steele and Balding, 2014).

A case from the files of the author illustrates the problem of stutters and mixtures.

CASE 4.5   Mixture; Stutter; Trace DNA

A woman reversing out of her driveway claimed a man known to her opened fire on her car and it was riddled with bullets. The bullets passed through the car and she was hit by shattered glass and taken to hospital with minor injuries. She identified the man as the shooter and he pleaded not guilty at trial to attempted murder.

A gun was located by police at the house of the girlfriend of the accused. Trace DNA was obtained from the gun and said to comprise three contributors, including the accused. It was considered to be eight million times in favour of DNA matching the accused contributing to the mixture than if the DNA did not. The defence claimed that there was no evidence that the accused was the shooter and there was no motive.

The mixture DNA from the gun was a partial profile and poor quality. Initially there were two 'unknowns', as well as the accused, considered contributing DNA to the mixture. A reference sample from the girlfriend was then analyzed, and it was found it was one billion times more likely that she contributed DNA than if she did not. The extra peaks in the mixture profile that could not be explained by the DNA of the accused, his girlfriend and another person were claimed by the laboratory to be stutter, and not alleles. However, the statistical program considered these peaks as potential alleles.

The judge did not allow the DNA evidence. The jury acquitted the accused.

Recommendation 6 from the DNA commission of the International Society of Forensic Genetics (Gill et al., 2006) is that if the crime profile is a major/minor mixture where minor alleles are the same height as stutters of major alleles, then stutters and minor alleles are indistinguishable. This recommendation has not been supplanted.

Partial Profiles

Degradation may often be observed from the EPG. The longer fragments of DNA are more likely to be affected first, and the consequence is the failure to amplify fully or at all compared to the shorter fragments of DNA. This may result in the 'ski slope' effect observed in an EPG where the peaks towards the right-hand side of the diagram are noticeably smaller in height than the ones towards the left-hand side. Sometimes, the larger fragments are so low in peak height that they cannot be discerned from the baseline, and thus only a *partial* DNA profile can be designated.

Degraded samples are particularly a problem in mixtures as the two or more samples that compose a mixture DNA profile may have different levels of degradation, and thus there may be different interpretations by analysts.

Figure 4.6 shows a degraded DNA profile, with some of the loci having no discernible alleles present.

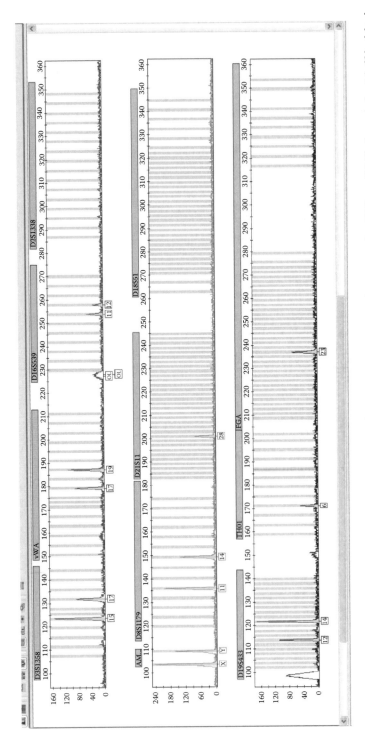

FIGURE 4.6   A DNA profile showing degradation/inhibition of DNA; no results at two loci D2 and D18. An artefact 'off ladder' peak is marked as 'OL'. All peaks are low in height (from vertical scale).

Statistical Evaluation

A statistical weight of evidence is premised on the designation of alleles in the interpretation of the DNA profile, and some methods use assumptions of the number of contributors. The statistical evaluation of DNA profiles has traditionally been based on the frequencies of alleles in the relevant population. The calculations are straightforward when there is no ambiguity in the profile. But mixtures, when a major and a minor contributor cannot be separated, partial profiles and low amounts of DNA introduce problems that are still unresolved in the forensic science community.

A recent paper discussed an English appeals court decision (Gill et al., 2014). The authors outlined the problems that may result in interpretation of complex mixtures. The paper discussed that it appeared scientists could report complex mixture DNA profiles using just their subjective personal experience of casework and observations, in order to apply an expression of the rarity of an evidential sample.

The forensic community is moving towards the implementation of new methods to interpret complex DNA mixture profiles. Chapters 5 and 6 will further discuss these issues.

Relatives

Kinship analysis, a subset which is paternity testing, is usually treated as a separate area within forensic genetics. Other uses include the identification of missing persons and disaster victim identification. There are cases where kinship and crime overlap such as mixtures where the contributors may be related.

DNA Databases

Today national and regional DNA databases are in use in many countries through statutory legislation – these countries include the United Kingdom, Canada, Australia and the United States. These databases have provided many cold 'hits' for unknown samples left at a crime scene. Thus, as well as comparison with provided reference samples, biological evidential samples may also be compared to DNA databases in order to find a potential 'match' with a convicted offender.

There are approximately six million records in the UK National DNA Database, but it is no longer the largest database in the world. China has more than 32 million records as of November 2014, more than twice the size of the U.S. database, greater than 13 million samples (Gill et al., 2015). It is interesting to note that as a proportion of the population, the United Kingdom still ranks the highest with approximately 10% of the population on the national register, compared with approximately 4% of the U.S. population.

DNA profiling results are stored on computer in the form of an alphanumeric code that is based on each STR allele. Database matches are mainly through volume crime–type offences. A DNA database match or link may not represent an arrest or conviction but merely that a person 'may' have been at a scene. Extraneous profiles that are put on a DNA database means that it is more likely to get partial matches and more likely to get coincidental matches.

The DNA database is used primarily for intelligence. This is a separate exercise to the evaluation of the evidence in a specific case.

Cold Cases

Cases may be reinvestigated where the original biological evidence was equivocal, not discriminating, or where there was no suspect located. The scientific investigation is dependent on biological samples remaining in the cases. The innovation of DNA databasing has led to the solution of many of these cases.

A 'cold' case from Australia which had baffled police for nearly 12 years illustrates the potential of 'wearer' DNA belonging to the offender as well as blood from the victim on a pair of shoes – which was what caused the offender to discard them (Hall, 2011).

CASE 4.6   Cold Case; DNA Database; Wearer DNA

A heavily intoxicated 20-year-old man in Sydney, Australia, had become involved in a fight with a man with a goatee at a taxi rank in 1995. The young man was bashed and died from severe injuries in a nearby car park. Three unidentified men that came from a nearby nightclub were involved in the fracas.

The victim's wallet was stolen from his back pocket and his running shoes were taken. Two days later, a lawyer looked out of his office window and saw a pair of running shoes on the awning – his office was a few blocks from the murder scene. The lawyer gave the shoes to the police and the DNA from the blood on the outside of the shoes matched the DNA of the victim in the bashing. The inside tongue of the shoes was sampled, and another DNA profile was obtained (the 'wearer' DNA) which did not match anyone on the database. But it matched the DNA from the blood found on the inside of the victim's back pocket. The police theorized the offender had injured his knuckles in the altercation and discarded his shoes, and taken the victim's, because his own were covered in blood.

During 2008 Darren Paul Smith was arrested by Queensland police (another state) for being drunk while riding a bicycle that he had stolen. The offence of larceny in Queensland required him to submit a sample for DNA profiling on the database. When placed on the national database, it matched the DNA profile from the tongue of the running shoes and the back pocket of the trousers from the victim. The defence argued that the DNA in question came from transfer as the relevant exhibits were put together in the same exhibit bag. The accused was found guilty by a jury and sentenced to a minimum of 18 years in prison.

There should be proper audits in cold cases. The exhibits may have been initially examined in conditions lacking the strict contamination mitigation measures used today. This is because transfer of minute quantities of DNA was not considered before the 1990s. The problems with transfer of DNA and context have been discussed in Chapters 2 and 3.

References

Alberts, B., Johnson, A. and Lewis, J. 2002. *Molecular Biology of the Cell*, 4th edn. Garland Science: New York.

Balding, D. and Buckleton, J. 2009. Interpreting low template DNA profiles. *Forensic Sci. Int. Genet.* 4: 1–10.

Ballantyne, K., Poy, A. and van Oorschot, R.A. 2013. Environmental DNA monitoring: Beware of the transition to more sensitive typing methodologies. *Aust. J. Forensic Sci.* 45(3): 323–340.

Butler, J. 2012. *Advanced Topics in Forensic DNA Typing: Methodology.* Elsevier Academic Press: San Diego, CA.

Caddy, B., Taylor, G.R. and Linacre, A.M.T. 2008. A review of the science of low template DNA analysis (Home Office Forensic Regulation Unit). Available at: https://www.gov.uk/government/uploads/system/uploads/attachment_data/file/117556/Review_of_Low_Template_DNA_1.pdf/, accessed 21 November 2015.

Gill, P., Bleka, O. and Egeland, T. 2014. Does an English appeal court ruling increase the risks of miscarriage of justice when complex DNA profiles are searched against the national DNA database? *Forensic Sci. Int. Genet.* 13: 167–175.

Gill, P., Brenner, C.H., Buckleton, J. et al. 2006. DNA commission of the international society of forensic genetics: Recommendations on the interpretation of mixtures. *Forensic Sci. Int.* 160: 90–101.

Gill, P., Haned, H., Bleka, O. et al. 2015. Genotyping and Interpretation of STR-DNA: Low-template, mixtures and database matches – Twenty years of research and development. *Forensic Sci. Int. Genet.* 18: 100–107.

Gill, P. and Werrett, D. 1987. Exclusion of a man charged with murder by DNA fingerprinting. *Forensic Sci. Int.* 35: 145–148.

Hall, L. 2011. Drunken cyclist's DNA leads to cold case murder conviction. *Sydney Morning Herald*, 17 September 2011. Available at: http://www.smh.com.au/nsw/drunken-cyclists-dna-leads-to-cold-case-murder-conviction-20110916-1kdy7.htm, accessed 25 November 2015.

Honda, K. 2015. DNA analysis overturns the death sentence of a condemned criminal held in custody for 48 years. *Forensic Sci. Int. Genet.* 16: e5–e6.

Innocence Project. Available at: http://www.innocenceproject.org, accessed 25 November 2015.

Peel, C. and Gill, P. 2014. Attribution of DNA profiles to body fluid stains. *Int. Congr. Ser.* 1261: 53–55.

Rennison, A. 2012. Report into the circumstances of a complaint received from the Greater Manchester Police on 7 March 2012 regarding DNA evidence provided by LGC Forensics. Forensic Science Regulator, U.K. Available at: https://www.gov.uk/government/publications/forensic-science-regulators-report-on-the-dna-contamination-case-at-lgc-forensics, accessed 25 November 2015.

SWGDAM (Scientific Working Group on DNA Analysis Methods). 2010. Interpretation guidelines for autosomal STR typing by forensic DNA testing laboratories. Available on the FBI website at: http://www.fbi.gov/about-us/lab/codis/swgdam.pdf, accessed 25 November 2015.

Steele, C. and Balding, D. 2014. Statistical evaluation of forensic DNA profiling evidence. *Annu. Rev. Stat. Appl.* 1: 361–384.

Taupin, J. and Cwiklik, C. 2010. *Scientific Protocols for the Forensic Examination of Clothing.* CRC Press: Boca Raton: FL.

Chapter **5**

Statistics

Introduction

The ultimate power of DNA profiling is its power of discrimination. DNA is 'individual' to a person; only identical twins (or identical triplets or even more) will have the same DNA. However, the whole of the DNA from a person cannot be analyzed in a DNA profile. A limited number of areas on the DNA molecule are examined in forensic science laboratories.

Further, it is not possible to DNA profile every person in a particular country. Sampling statistics are used to extrapolate the DNA profile from a small database (sometimes less than a few hundred people) to a population at large.

The interpretation of DNA profiles when there is a 'match' between profiles requires the determination of a probability – the chance of observing a second copy of *that DNA profile* in a certain population. There has been much debate in the forensic literature about how this probability should be derived.

Just the word *statistics* can introduce difficulty in any trial. With the advent of DNA profiling and its inherent reliance on statistics, various bodies have recognized this problem and produced guidelines. A U.S. judicial body has provided a manual on scientific evidence (U.S. Federal Judicial Centre, 2011). The Royal Statistical Society in London has also produced two practitioner guides (Aitken et al., 2010; Puch-Solis et al., 2012) on statistical analysis, the second guide focusing on DNA evidence.

Lord Ernest Rutherford was a Nobel Prize winning physicist from early last century and famed for the elegant simplicity of his experiments. He has been quoted as saying 'If your experiment needs statistics, you ought to do a better experiment'. The increasing age of scientific complexity and the acceptance of 'black boxes' in computer systems sometimes overwhelm the importance of the simple experiment.

The probative 'value' of DNA in a trial is a different concept to the statistical match of DNA profiles. The probative value is determined by the court.

A conviction has been based on DNA evidence alone (e.g. the Farah Jama case, Case 2.1; Vincent, 2010). This has been recognized as an approach which can present difficulties.

A judgement from Australia, and quoted in a case relying solely on DNA evidence, has explained the caution required in such situations (*R v. Fletcher*, 1998; Vincent, 2010).

CASE 5.1   Meaning of a DNA Profile Match; Caution

The judge said 'the DNA matching, if proved beyond reasonable doubt, does not prove that the accused is the offender. The evidence only fails to prove he is not the offender. The only inference which can be drawn from a match beyond reasonable doubt, together with the occurrence in the community, assuming you accept the percentage occurrences, which is not here challenged, is that it was possible that he was the person who had sexual intercourse with the deceased… if there is only DNA evidence and nothing else which you accept, you cannot convict the accused'.

Ensuring appropriate biochemical and genetic tests are performed will mean that the best result is obtained. It is better to analyze further or replicate stains on the item, for example, and to try and obtain a better result than to perform complicated statistical analyses on a suboptimal result.

Statistical Interpretation and Wording

How the statistical 'meaning' of a DNA result is conveyed in a report and testimony may be crucial. What a statistic means and just as importantly, what it does not mean, should be conveyed as simply as possible.

The 'prosecutor's fallacy' (sometimes called transposition of the conditional) and how to avoid it has been described in scientific and legal texts over many years. It bears repeating here as it is illustrative of a major problem. The prime example is a case from the United Kingdom (Aitken et al., 2010; *R v. Deen*, 1995). This was an early DNA case where the random match probability (RMP) of a DNA profile was quoted as one in three million.

Prosecutor: So the likelihood of this being any other man but Andrew Deen is one in 3 million?

Expert: In 3 million, yes.

Prosecutor: You are a scientist … doing this research … a jury are going to be asked whether they are sure that it is Andrew Deen who committed this particular rape in relation to Miss W. On the figure which you have established according to your research, the possibility of it being anybody else being one in 3 million what is your conclusion?

Expert: My conclusion is that the semen originated from Andrew Deen.

Prosecutor: Are you sure of that?

Expert: Yes.

The basic fallacy is contained in the first question when the attorney asks the probability of the accused being the source of the DNA profile, rather than the probability of the DNA profile.

Having been asked the wrong question, the expert in *R v. Deen* then confounded this fallacy by saying the accused was the source of the stain.

The prosecution fallacy, or transposing the conditional, is simply described in the two following statements (Aitken et al., 2010):

1. If I am a monkey, I have two arms and legs.
2. If I have two arms and legs, I am a monkey.

The first proposition is a non-transferable conditional proposition (conditional because of the 'if'). The second transferred proposition is clearly nonsense.

The transposition of the conditional was also discussed by the Court of Appeal in the United Kingdom (*R v. Doheny and Adams*, 1997). A conviction was overturned on this appeal. It explains the situation again:

> Only one person in a million will have a DNA profile which matches that of the crime stain.
> The defendant has a DNA profile which matches the crime stain.
> Ergo, there is a million to one probability that the defendant left the crime stain and is guilty of the crime.

A final example comes from another appeals court in the United Kingdom (*R v. Gordon*, 1997). The frequencies of the DNA profiles were calculated to be about 1 in 10 million and 1 in 17 million in the population. An expert witness testified that they were sure of the match between the semen samples and the appellant's blood. This is called a source probability error (Aitken et al., 2010). Although apparently there was an extreme unlikelihood of a random match with the DNA profile, this cannot infer a definitive source (such as from the accused). This is a more particular example of transposing the conditional.

Concept of 'Uniqueness'

It is not possible to identify a particular individual as the donor of the genetic material from whom the DNA was produced. DNA is essentially probabilistic. Even if DNA is unique to an individual, more than one person could share the *same DNA profile*.

Probability is concerned with uncertainty. There have been rulings on admissibility especially by the Court of Appeal in English courts of law where it has been stated that DNA is always a matter of probability. These have been called 'The Adams Family' of appeals (Aitken et al., 2010).

Only impossible events can ever be assigned a value of zero. The interesting 'Cromwell's rule' refers to Oliver Cromwell's plea to save his life to the General Assembly of the Church of Scotland on 3 August 1650: 'I beseech you, in the bowels of Christ, think it possible that you may be mistaken' (Aitken et al., 2010; quoted from Oxford Dictionary of Quotations; 1979).

One misconception is that there is an exact answer to the question of probability of a particular DNA profile given that it came from someone other than the defendant. But the probability of an event is inevitably conditioned by the assumptions that are made, and there is no situation in which one can have a probability without making at least one assumption.

There is a growing realization that all scientific evidence is probabilistic and no current forensic technology supports unique identification of individuals. DNA is different only because it is explicit about the probability.

Statistical Approaches

It is difficult to understand probabilities as a concept. It is easier to think in terms of natural frequencies. For a DNA profile, this leads to the question, how many people in the population could have contributed to the profile?

The *random match probability* explanation is one of the simplest in DNA profiling statistics, but textbooks caution even its interpretation. It is not the probability of obtaining another DNA match in the population. The RMP is the probability of obtaining a match 'in one go'. It is not conditioned, and it is not the probability that at least one other member of the population of interest will produce a match.

Three different types of statistical approaches are used in forensic evidence, in general – not just DNA (Buckleton et al., 2005). These are

1. Frequentist approach
2. Likelihood ratio (LR) approach
3. Full Bayesian approach

Classical hypothesis testing gives one hypothesis (or model) a preferred status. This is called the 'null hypothesis' and considers evidence *against* it. The Bayes factor is a Bayesian alternative to classical hypothesis testing (named after Reverend Bayes, a Scottish mathematician).

The Bayesian approach is based on at least three ideas: (1) It is necessary to consider an alternative proposition in any evaluation of a probability. (2) Scientific interpretation is based on 'what is the probability of the evidence, given the proposition'. (3) The interpretation is also 'conditioned' on the framework of circumstances. The LR is obtained from the Bayes theorem.

So far the use of LRs and Bayes theorem in forensic evidence other than DNA has not been favoured in court. It is interesting to note that a 'full' Bayesian approach to the statistical evaluation is used in some 'expert systems' in computer simulations (see section 'Expert Computer Systems'). A full Bayesian analysis uses the weight of evidence as to the posterior probability that the suspect is the donor of a particular stain. Such an approach requires the specification of *prior probabilities*, or at least their ratio, which in turn has discouraged many.

Single Contributor Profiles

The simplest statistical calculations are for a complete (or full) DNA profile, considered to come from one person only.

Evidence yielding full single-source DNA profiles will use either one of two statistical approaches by the reporting forensic laboratory:

1. *Random match probabilities* – based on allele frequency estimates
2. *LR* – conditional probability ratio based on frequencies calculated from the first hypothesis versus the alternate hypothesis

A RMP is the chance of a random DNA profile match within a given population and is the reciprocal of the DNA profile frequency. A DNA profile frequency is estimated by determining the genotype frequency for each locus and then multiplying the frequency across all loci (areas on the molecule).

The probability of inclusion (PI) is also termed random man not excluded (RMNE). The converse is the probability of exclusion (PE).

The *ratio* of the probabilities of the evidence under two or more alternative hypotheses about the source(s) of the profile is called the likelihood ratio. The LR is becoming the most preferred approach worldwide. If the LR is greater than one, then the evidence supports the first (or prosecution) proposition; if it is less than one, it supports the second (or defence) proposition.

The statistics for both approaches are based on the same frequencies. These are the frequencies of each 'allele' or 'STR (short tandem repeat)' at 16 or more areas on the DNA molecule. It involves multiplication, which gives rise to the high values often observed.

An early case in the history of DNA profiling that used both the RMP and the LR was from the United States. The accused was O.J. Simpson (Case 1.3; Thompson, 1996; Weir, 1995). The prosecution wished to use the LR and the defence wished to use the RMNE, but the outcome was that the court heard both methods.

There is a summary of the advantages and disadvantages of each approach (Clayton and Buckleton, 2005), and a full discussion of the various methods to interpret evidence can be found in comprehensive texts (for example Buckleton et al., 2005). The methods based on RMNE are easier to understand and explain especially in a court situation. However, an unrealistically simple model of DNA evidence is used. This is why it is restricted to, so far, *unambiguous* profiles.

The DNA commission of the International Society for Forensic Genetics (Gill et al., 2006, 2012) recommends LRs, whether they are difficult to convey or not.

New ways of thinking are needed to explain statistics in court. Perhaps the past approach (as in the O.J. Simpson case) of using a variety of methods to explain data should be considered, rather than a single dogmatic approach.

RMNE Approach

The combined probability of inclusion (CPI) and the combined probability of exclusion (CPE) calculations are used by some laboratories to indicate the statistical significance of results. CPI is the percentage of the population that can be included in a profile; CPE is the percentage of the population that can be excluded from a profile. The CPI and CPE calculations are closely related: CPI is calculated by multiplying the probabilities of inclusion from each locus, and CPE is calculated by subtracting the value obtained from the CPI calculation from 1 (that is, 1 − CPI). This terminology is often observed in Y-STR typing and mitochondrial DNA reports because LRs cannot be performed for these analyses (see Chapter 7).

The PE, or the RMNE, or the complementary PI, entails a 'binary' view of alleles in a DNA profile. This means that alleles are only present or absent. Further, if they are present, then they are observed.

If there are alleles where there is a possibility of 'stochastic' or random sampling effects and perhaps the allele may not be observed, sometimes laboratories omit from the calculation the inconvenient (non-matching) loci (Gill et al., 2006). Such a calculation *incorrectly* implies that among the 'random men' considered for comparison, only the same loci would be used for inclusion/exclusion as those considered for the present suspect (see Chapter 6 for further discussion on low-level DNA).

Likelihood Ratio

The LR in DNA evidence has been used for many years in the United Kingdom, Europe and Australia.

The LR is a ratio of probabilities of a piece of evidence – considering two different alternatives. It uses conditional probabilities, and thus assumptions.

There is additional complexity in trying to ensure that LR interpretations are conducted without fallacious reasoning (transposition of the conditional is exacerbated).

A conditional probability can be stated as follows: Given that A occurs, what is the probability that B occurs? That is, the probability of B is conditioned on the event A occurring.

The hypotheses are conditioned statements that describe the alternative prosecution and defence hypotheses, described as Hp and Hd, respectively.

The LR equals PrE/Hp divided by Pr E/Hd; a ratio of two probabilities of evidence conditioned on two scenarios.

The probability of the evidence given the hypothesis should not be translated to the probability of the hypothesis itself. This can be a trap in the use of LRs.

Major and minor contributors may sometimes not be separated by the scientist in the interpretation step of the DNA profile (at least by the analyst). This step may be left to a computer 'expert system' designed to 'deconvolute mixtures'.

The simple evaluation of a single contributor major profile (and a trace minor DNA profile) may be mired in a large number of LRs in a report and end up confusing the reader. A case with numerous small LRs, but one extremely large one, indicated a major contributor – although this was not stated (from author's case files).

CASE 5.2   Likelihood Ratio; Many Values

A couple in an abusive de facto relationship had a small party with friends and relatives involving alcohol. The young woman was found bashed to death at the premises. The partner of the deceased could not remember what happened.

There was blood and pieces of human tissue on an outdoor piece of furniture. This biological matter was stated to have DNA that matched the victim with a LR of 100 billion in favour of the proposition that the victim was the source. Trace DNA from other areas of the furniture were stated to have LRs that flipped between support for the prosecution hypothesis (LR = 10) and support for the defence hypothesis (LR = 900) regarding the accused. There were three contributors to the trace DNA profile; there was a LR of 100 billion in favour of the hypothesis of the victim contributing to the trace DNA.

Apart from the apparent transposing of the conditional (probability of the proposition, instead of the evidence), there were three contributors to the trace

DNA profile. There was one 'unknown' contributor to the trace samples. The DNA profiles were not provided to the defence. However, it could be inferred that the major proportion or component of DNA from all the samples was from the victim, and there was a trace contributor(s) who could have been anyone. The accused and the victim lived together, and blood from various areas of the furniture piece was not disputed.

The DNA was not in issue at the trial.

A LR is the strength of evidence statement – in answer to a specific question defined by the prosecution and defence hypotheses. The value of a LR cannot be interpreted without understanding those hypotheses.

The LR only compares the relative likelihood of two hypotheses, *but that does not preclude both hypotheses as false.*

Mixtures

The larger the number of contributors, the more complex the DNA profile; when there are four or more contributors, generally a large portion of the population would be included in the profile. Most laboratories do not attempt to perform interpretation on four or more contributors to a mixed DNA profile unless a major contributor can be determined.

The interpretation of a mixed DNA profile is relatively simple when the following criteria apply (Word, 2011):

- The DNA is from only two sources.
- The two sources are unrelated and have no or few shared alleles.
- The ratio of the amount of DNA contributed by each of the two sources is adequate for interpretation of both sources.
- The appropriate amount of DNA was amplified resulting in all alleles for both sources being above the analytical threshold of the laboratory.
- No degradation, inhibition, primer variants, etc. are present to affect peak heights and the apparent DNA ratio.

- All stutter peaks and any other artefacts are below the analytical threshold or clearly distinguishable as artefacts.

Significant alteration to any of these parameters will likely make the mixture interpretation more complex; a combination of several alterations generally confounds the interpretation significantly (Word, 2011).

'Masking' of peaks (sharing of alleles) is a common occurrence in mixtures. This is because a contributor reference DNA profile to a mixture may have a particular allele or value at a locus that is the same as another contributor DNA profile. The contributions may be additive if they are similar in amount or they may not be observed if one contributor has donated depreciably less DNA than the other(s).

A major/minor separation of contributors may not be possible. It is necessary to make an assessment in relation to the balance of peak heights and mixture proportion (Gill et al., 2006).

RMNE Approach to Mixtures

So far, the RMNE approach cannot deal effectively with ambiguous profiles. Mixtures may have each contributor at a low level summing up to what is perceived to be a total good quality of DNA. The RMNE approach can only cope with loci that do not show, or potentially have, alleles that may have 'dropped out'. It needs to be assured that the DNA may be a proper representation of the person who deposited it.

It has been recognized that the RMNE approach, such as the CPI calculation, should not be suspect driven. There has been recent research in the RMNE approach to DNA profiles that may be partial and ambiguous. This holds promise as the RMNE statistic is simpler to explain and understand; the source codes are freely available (Christophe et al., 2015).

Likelihood Ratio Approach to Mixtures

Statistical calculations using LRs can potentially cope with ambiguous profiles, including artefacts produced as a consequence of

low levels of DNA or stutter in the copying process, treating artefacts in a probabilistic manner.

A case illustrating assumptions in the number of contributors
is described in the following text (from the author's case files).

CASE 5.3 Likelihood Ratio; Numerous Contributors; Assumptions

A woman was found dead from a brutal bashing in a
park. She was known to have occasionally taken money
for sexual favours. Fingernail scrapings were obtained
at autopsy. Two men S1 and S2 were charged with her
murder.

One fingernail had a DNA mixture that was stated to
appear to originate from four people. LRs were derived
through an expert computer system. It was stated to
be approximately 100 billion times more likely that S1,
the victim and two unknowns contributed to the DNA
versus the victim and three unknowns. It was approximately 2.4 billion times more likely the profile would
occur if S2, the victim and two unknowns contributed
versus the victim and three unknowns.

An interpretation of the DNA profile indicated at
least five contributors. Furthermore, the expert computer system that was used to deconvolute the mixture
had five contributors in the evaluation – the peaks were
considered to be alleles as well as stutter.

The time of deposition of the DNA could not be correlated with the time of death, and there was a direction
of acquittal for the accused S1. The second accused S2
had previously pleaded.

The LR is initially suspect driven, dependent on a scenario including the suspect.

The following literature article describes a case that was dis-
guised by the authors in order to conceal the circumstances
(Buckleton et al., 2014).

CASE 5.4   Likelihood Ratio; Numerous Suspects; Numerous Statistics

There was a murder of four related people. A bloodstain was recovered, associated with the accused, which could be explained by the DNA of all four deceased. However, there were 27 relatives that were sampled as references. Each of the 27 reference samples individually formed LRs. The Hp or prosecution hypothesis was that the DNA came from the reference and three unknowns, and for the defence hypothesis Hd, the DNA came from four unknown people. There were 27 LRs of which 7 were greater than 1.

Given the number of related people, the article did not think these LRs unexpected. The problem was that several of the seven non-excluded people were overseas and not plausible donors to the mixed bloodstain.

The article suggested that the overseas relatives should never have been considered. However, the large number of LRs and their insensitivity to the propositions demonstrate that consideration of just one LR, greater than one, may not tell the story.

The article emphasized that close attention should be given to the formulation of propositions.

Cases 5.2 through 5.4 show the problems when using the LR when there are numerous alternative propositions and numerous contributors. How to explain this simply is still a matter of debate.

It may be necessary to consider different propositions at various stages of the analysis. There is no reason why multiple pairs of propositions may not be evaluated (Buckleton et al., 2005; Gill and Haned, 2013). The DNA result itself may indicate that different explanations are possible.

The data produced from expert computer systems need to be in accord with the number of contributors, or the hypotheses, proposed by the scientist.

There is a common misconception that the numbers of contributors under the prosecution hypothesis and the defence hypothesis should be the same, but there is no reason for this to be so.

A range of LRs in an exploratory framework may be denoted in casework. An exploratory approach has been recommended for LRs that provides a way of testing the reliability of the obtained results (Gill and Haned, 2013).

Performance Tests

The variation in a provided LR statistic for a crime sample requires assessment. How does this statistic perform?

It is desirable to know the answer to the question, what is the chance that a randomly chosen non-contributor would generate a likelihood ratio at least as high as the one obtained for the suspect?

Performance tests, such as simulated testing of non-contributor profiles, can be used to estimate such a probability for a given result with a specific mixture (Gill and Haned, 2013). This is an attempt to show any distance between a *suspect-orientated* LR and a set of non-contributor LRs.

This type of testing is important when a LR is obtained for two suspects in the prosecution hypothesis scenario. A single LR cannot be applied to determine individual strengths of evidence per contributor (Gill et al., 2015).

The LR is a holistic statistic that cannot distinguish between contributors within the construct. Their relative contributions may be disproportionate. Non-contributor tests are used to 'dissect' the propositions. The following article describes an 'example case' (Gill and Haned, 2013; Haned et al., 2013).

CASE 5.5   Trace DNA; Mixture; Two Suspects; Likelihood Ratio; Non-Contributor Testing

A swab was taken from a female victim. Two male suspects S1 and S2 were accused of an offence on the victim, but both denied an offence. A low-level DNA profile was obtained from the swab from two or three people.

The evidence was evaluated as a LR and 'exploratory' as it was not obvious what the correct hypotheses were.

The LR calculated for both the suspects for the prosecution hypothesis (numerator) appeared to support the inclusion of the second suspect S2. However, when non-contributor tests were performed, this showed that S2 in the model acted no better than a 'random man'.

Non-contributor tests supported the contribution of S1.

The LR calculated from a complex proposition cannot be used as concurrent against all proposed contributors unless evaluated or *dissected*.

Expert Computer Systems

Expert systems have been developed as specialized software to interpret complex DNA profiles. They typically automate calculations of statistics that are relevant to different applications of forensic DNA profiling such as kinship testing, disaster victim identification and the analysis of crime samples.

A number of expert systems have recently become available and have been introduced in casework in forensic laboratories. There should be the normal process of validation of any novel test in a laboratory. Chapter 9 discusses this issue.

Some systems rely on assumptions not easily verified. Some programs also perform full Bayesian analysis. The debate regarding the use of full Bayesian models has not been resolved. A recent review (Gill et al., 2015) discusses the issues particularly in relation to low-level DNA profiles, and low-template concepts are discussed in the next chapter.

Population Databases

Population databases are different from intelligence databases and are referred to as 'frequency databases'. They are used to estimate the frequency of an allele in a population. Allele frequencies differ between indigent peoples, so it is usual practice to collect databases for the major ethnic groups that comprise common population groups of a country.

References

Aitken, C., Roberts, P. and Jackson, G. 2010. *Practitioner Guide 1 – Fundamentals of Probability and Statistical Evidence in Criminal Proceedings*. Royal Statistical Society: London, U.K. (available online).

Balding, D.J. and Nichols, R.A. 1994. DNA profile match probability calculation: How to allow for population stratification, relatedness, database selection and single bands. *Forensic Sci. Int.* 64: 125.

Buckleton, J. 2005. A framework for interpreting evidence in Buckleton. In *Forensic DNA Evidence Interpretation*, Buckelton, J., Triggs, C.M., and Walsh, S.J. (eds.), pp. 27–63. CRC Press: Boca Raton, FL.

Buckleton, J., Bright, J., Taylor, D. et al. 2014. Helping formulate propositions in forensic DNA analysis. *Sci. Justice* 54: 258–261.

Buckleton, J., Curran, J. and Gill, P. 2007. Towards understanding the effects of uncertainty in the number of contributors to DNA stains. *Forensic Sci. Int. Genet.* 1: 20–28.

Buckleton, J., Triggs, C.M. and Walsh, C.J. 2005. *Forensic DNA Evidence Interpretation*. CRC Press: Boca Raton, FL.

Christophe, V.N., Dieter, D. and Filip, V.N. 2015. Effect of multiple allelic drop-outs in forensic RMNE calculations. *Forensic Sci. Int.: Gen.* 19: 243–249.

Clayton, T. and Buckleton, J. 2005. Mixtures. In: *Forensic DNA Evidence Interpretation*, Buckelton, J., Triggs, C.M. and Walsh, S.J. (eds.), pp. 217–274. CRC Press: Boca Raton, FL.

Gill, P., Brenner, C.H., Buckleton, J.S. et al. 2006. DNA commission of the International Society of Forensic Genetics: Recommendations on the interpretation of mixtures. *Forensic Sci. Int.* 160: 90–101.

Gill, P., Gusmao, L., Haned, H. et al. 2012. DNA Commission of the International Society of Forensic Genetics: Recommendations on the evaluation of STR typing results that may include drop out and/or drop-in using probabilistic methods. *Forensic Sci. Int. Genet.* 6: 679–688.

Gill, P. and Haned, H. 2013. A new methodological framework to interpret complex DNA profiles using likelihood ratios. *Forensic Sci. Int. Genet.* 7: 251–263.

Gill, P., Haned, H. and Bleka, O. 2015. Genotyping and interpretation of STR-DNA: Low-template, mixtures and database matches – Twenty years of research and development. *Forensic Sci. Int. Genet.* 18: 100–117.

Haned, H., Dorum, G., Egeland, T. et al. 2013. On the meaning of the likelihood ratio: Is a large number always an indication of strength of evidence? *Forensic Sci. Int. Genet. Suppl.* 4: e176–e177.

National Research Council. 2009. *Strengthening Forensic Science in the United States: A Path Forward*. National Academy Press: Washington, DC.

Puch-Solis, R., Roberts, P., Pope, S. et al. 2012. *Practitioner Guide 2 – Assessing the Probative Value of DNA Evidence*. Royal Statistical Society: London, U.K. (available online).

SWGDAM Guidelines. 2010. SWGDAM interpretation guidelines for autosomal STR typing by forensic DNA testing laboratories. Available on the FBI website at: http://www.fbi.gov/about-us/lab/codis/swgdam.pdf, 25 November 2015.

The Queen v. Deen. 1995. CA The Times 10 January 1994.

The Queen v. Doheny and Adams. 1997. 1 Cr App R 369 CA.

The Queen v. Fletcher. 1998. 2 QR 437.

The Queen v. Gordon. 1997. 1 Cr App R 290, CA.

Thompson, W.C. 1996. DNA evidence in the O.J. Simpson trial. *Univ. Colorado Law Rev.* 67(Fall): 827–857.

U.S. Federal Judicial Centre. 2011. *Reference Manual on Scientific Evidence*, 3rd edn. The National Academies Press: Washington, DC.

Vincent, H.F. 2010. Inquiry into the circumstances that led to the conviction of Mr Farah Abdulkadir Jama. Victorian Government Printer: Melbourne, Victoria, Australia.

Weir, B.S. 1995. DNA statistics in the Simpson matter. *Nat. Genet.* 11: 365–368.

Word, C.J. 2011. Mixture Interpretation: Why is it sometimes so hard? Available at: http://www.promega.com/resources/articles/profiles-in-dna/2011, 25 November 2015.

Chapter **6**

Low Template, Low Level or Low Copy Number DNA

Introduction

Ever smaller amounts of DNA from deposits at a crime scene are interpreted today, much smaller than was originally envisioned in 1985 when DNA profiling was first implemented. These small deposits may not be associated with a visible stain, for example trace DNA deposited through handling. The DNA deposited may not be able to be associated with a particular body matter such as blood.

Sometimes the amount of DNA available for testing is low because the DNA has degraded through poor environmental conditions (such as heat and humidity). It may be inhibited and not amplify properly due to chemicals in the substrate, such as the dye from denim jeans.

These small amounts may be *below* the levels of DNA recommended by DNA typing kits (even newer kits such as Identifiler and PowerPlex21). The recommended amount of DNA is more than 250 pg (250 picograms, a trillionth of 1 g) or one quarter of a nanogram (a nanogram is one billionth of 1 g). New biochemistry has increased the sensitivity of DNA tests. It is possible to generate profiles from as little as 20 pg of DNA – less than one tenth of the recommended amount – which is the equivalent of about three cells.

The tests are so sensitive now that forensic laboratories are often analyzing low template DNA without necessarily being explicit that this is the case. The once controversial analysis of low template or low copy number (LCN) amounts of DNA is considered to be the routine (Gill et al., 2015).

A good-quality DNA profile may result from a less than optimal DNA quantity as measured in a quantification test. Conversely, a poor-quality profile may result from a sufficient quantity of DNA. It is the quality of the profile that is the crucial factor.

It is accepted now that when a low template DNA profile is encountered, it is no longer certain that the observed alleles in the sample faithfully reflect the trace donor's genotype (their fragments of DNA). What is sampled, and then what is produced through the technical process, may not reflect the DNA composition in the body of the donor human.

Amplification of random sampling effects may result in missing alleles from the donor because the reaction may have failed for that allele (termed 'dropout'). Extra alleles may appear due to tiny fragments of contaminating DNA (termed 'dropin').

Ambiguity and uncertainty from these effects in low level DNA profiles has created difficulties in subsequent statistical interpretations of the profile. How the uncertainty is measured, or whether the profile should even be interpreted, has caused controversy.

This chapter will attempt to discuss some of the problems due to the analysis of these small amounts and how the forensic literature and court processes have considered them.

History
Enhancement Techniques

An increased number of amplification cycles in the process was tried to detect lower levels of DNA than was previously possible. These techniques to increase sensitivity were first employed in the mid- to late 1990s and called 'low copy number', low copies of the DNA molecule. Other methods used to increase sensitivity have been post-amplification purification and reduced volume for amplification (Butler, 2012).

One of the first articles describing LCN suggested caution in the interpretation of the resulting DNA profiles. It was proposed that a clause should be inserted in expert statements cautioning the court on the lack of interpretative information such as transfer and persistence studies when determining the value of low level DNA (Gill et al., 2000). This recommendation has *not* been supplanted.

Issues surrounding the interpretation of DNA profiles using low level analytical techniques such as LCN were brought to the attention of the scientific community, and the public domain after this type of evidence was questioned in the Omagh bombing case in Northern Ireland 2007 by the presiding judge (*R v. Hoey,* 2007; Case 1.7).

CASE 6.1   Low Level DNA; Method Validation

A car bomb killed and injured many people in Northern Ireland in 1998. Sean Hoey was charged in 2005 after it was alleged his DNA was found on bomb timers collected during the crime scene examination. The technique of LCN was used to analyze the DNA.

Justice Weir concluded that low template DNA techniques had not been appropriately validated by the scientific community. In his view, two articles published by the developers of the method were insufficient to validate the technique. Furthermore, Justice Weir said: 'The absence of an agreed protocol for the validation of scientific techniques prior to their being admitted in court is entirely unsatisfactory'.

Questions and concerns from this trial led the Association of Chief Police Officers in the United Kingdom to suspend the use of LCN profiling. The use of LCN DNA profiling recommenced after a government inquiry entitled 'a review of the science of low template DNA analysis' (Caddy et al., 2008).

The review is still pertinent today. It found that the laboratory methods were robust and fit for purpose, but confusion remained in the interpretation of these kinds of profiles.

The review found that the increase in sensitivity of the low level techniques may also increase stochastic (random) effects and the opportunity for detecting DNA not related to the alleged incident (either incidental or due to contamination). These processes confuse the outcome of such DNA profiling, and the process is usually repeated a small number of times. The random effects are not limited to increased cycle number 'but occur even with standard techniques (28 cycles) when using low template DNA', author emphasis. The amount of DNA considered low template was less than 200 pg.

An interesting comment was that 'There seems to be a feeling in some police forces that LTDNA is a panacea for the solution of all crime because of little understanding of the concepts and making submissions without consideration of contamination issues. Clearly there is a requirement to communicate the limitations of these procedures'. A recommendation was that a DNA profile using low template DNA techniques should be presented to a jury in a criminal trial with caveats – the nature of the starting material is unknown, the time at which the DNA was transferred cannot be inferred, and the opportunity for secondary transfer is increased in comparison to standard DNA profiling.

The review found that many laboratories had moved into the low template domain by dint of improved technology – without necessarily being explicit that this is the case. It was recommended there be further harmonization of standards for the production and interpretation of low template DNA data.

Note that the newer more discriminatory kits that examine more areas on the DNA molecule than previously are also more sensitive. The PowerPlex21 system that examines 21 markers (PowerPlex21 System, 2012) is more sensitive than previous kits but also uses more cycles in the amplification step – 30 cycles. This is instead of 28 cycles that was used in, for example, SGMplus (11 markers) or ProfilerPlus (10 markers).

The Caddy review noted that 'the International Society for Forensic Genetics' had published guidelines for low level DNA testing in 2006 (Gill et al., 2006). LCN in these guidelines was defined as the manifestation of stochastic (random) effects leading to allelic imbalance, dropout and increased prevalence of laboratory-based contamination. LCN was defined as usually associated with a low amount of DNA – less than 200 pg.

Improving Reliability of Results

There are two main areas where an attempt is made to improve the reliability of results when potentially working with low amounts of DNA and reduce any uncertainty. First, the amount of DNA recovered at the collection and extraction stages may be improved by employing specific laboratory techniques. Second, the uncertainty is assessed by accounting for stochastic (random) effects in the analysis with a consensus or statistical model.

Consensus Model

The 'consensus model' determines the DNA types via a consensus strategy from multiple DNA profiles produced from different amplifications. It was originally employed to facilitate the reporting of ambiguous DNA profiles that were subject to the phenomenon of dropout and dropin. A statistical model (below) was available to check calculations from consensus models (Gill et al., 2000) but was rarely used due to the complexity of the calculations and a lack of appropriate software.

The consensus amplification strategy became the core feature of low level DNA profiling. This concept was first published in 1996 (Taberlet et al., 1996), whereby an allele in a DNA profile was only recorded if it was observed at least twice. The standard practice was to amplify either two or three portions of a DNA extract (Caragine et al., 2009; Gill et al., 2000). It was noted that amplification results from a single test could be unreliable due to the stochastic amplification effects (Butler, 2012).

A UK court judgement described this consensus strategy and low level DNA profiles in general (*R v. Broughton*, 2010).

CASE 6.2   Low Copy Number;
Consensus Profiles; Reliability

The court held that evidence that was susceptible to random effects would be admissible where repeat testing (even a low number of repeat tests) produced consistent results. It was held that the science of LCN DNA was sufficiently well established to pass the ordinary tests of reliability and relevance. It would be wrong to deprive the justice system of the benefits to be gained from the new techniques and advances which it embodies, in cases where there is clear evidence that the profiles are sufficiently reliable.

The Italian appeals court in 2011 in the conviction of Amanda Knox and Raffaele Sollecito (Perugia murder case, discussed later) held that the failure to perform two amplifications from the blade of the alleged weapon, despite the quantity of DNA being very low, may be acceptable for initial investigative purposes '…but cannot be accepted when the genetic tests form the basis for evidence of guilt beyond any reasonable doubt' (Hellmann, 2011).

Statistical (Probabilistic) Model

A strategy for interpreting low level DNA profiles and accounting for stochastic variability was first introduced as the 'statistical model' (Gill et al., 2000). The statistical model can be used in two different ways. It can be used to develop a likelihood ratio per se, or it can be used to determine whether the consensus approach is safe under the circumstances described. It attempts to assess the probability of the replicates from all possible genotypes (Gill and Buckleton, 2010).

This approach is discussed in the next sections.

A case where neither model was used for low template DNA occurred a number of years ago (from author's case files).

CASE 6.3 Low Level DNA; Partial Profile; Mixture; Non-Concordance

A man was accused of threatening to kill another man by placing a pistol to his head. This pistol was later seized from the home of the accused, and the muzzle of the gun was swabbed to obtain 'trace DNA'.

A mixture DNA profile which had originated from at least three people was reported by the laboratory. The DNA profile from the complainant and the accused were not excluded from contributing to the mixture profile. A likelihood ratio statistic was reported considering two propositions – the DNA either originated from the accused, the complainant and one other unknown person or originated from the accused and two other unknown people. This statistic was 'conditioned' on the accused; that is it was assumed that the accused had contributed DNA to the mixture. It was estimated it would be over 1000 times more likely if the first proposition was true than if the second proposition was true.

The mixture was low level and DNA from the reference samples were only partially represented in the mixture. Consequently, there was only a partial match for both references. This partial match was *within* a locus so that there was non-concordance of the mixture alleles with the reference profiles.

The sample from the gun was not amplified twice so there was no consensus approach. A probabilistic approach was not used. It was not described in the expert statement that there was a partial match. The judge determined that the DNA evidence was not admissible.

'Dropout' of an allele was invoked to sustain the prosecution case above – that is not all of the reference profile alleles were present in the crime DNA. When this assumption is invoked, then an estimation of the dropout probabilities cannot be avoided (Balding and Buckleton, 2009).

For example, say the alleles detected at one locus in the mixture crime profile were 15, 17 and 18. If the reference profile had alleles of 15, 16, in order to propose that the reference DNA could have contributed, then 'dropout' of the 16 allele must be proposed.

Dropout and low level mixture DNA profiles (described as complex mixtures) are discussed further in the following text.

Low Template, Low Copy Number, Low Level

What is considered a 'low level' of DNA? An amount of less than 200 pg is one definition. Another is any DNA that falls below recommended thresholds for analysis at any stage (van Oorschot et al., 2010). Another explanation is a DNA peak that falls below a 'stochastic' or random sampling height in the DNA profile and thus may be subject to the random effects.

Two scientific authors (Gill and Buckleton, 2009) proposed there be no specific delineation for LCN or low template DNA due to the following: (1) the stochastic effects of low template DNA profiling are observed with all DNA profiling methods and (2) a definition based on a quantification value is not feasible (due to mixtures, degradation, inhibition). The transition between the two 'states' is gradual rather than sudden.

The authors of this article also 'abandoned' the LCN (low copy number term) and used the low template DNA term instead because of the confusion of the particular technique of extra amplification cycles, but the ambiguity effects are noticed regardless of technique (Balding and Buckleton, 2009).

The problem is the translation. Some laboratories do not state there is low template DNA from the crime scene sample because it is believed there is no definition for it. The author of this text considers 'ambiguous' a possible term to be applied for these types of profiles. Clearly, a DNA profile from a person used as a 'reference' profile should not be ambiguous. If it is (due to insufficient sample or limitation of the technique) then a laboratory should repeat the analysis to obtain a quality profile.

A UK appeals court heard two cases where low level techniques were used (*R v. Reed, Reed and Garmson*, 2009). The case of the brothers Reed is described as follows.

CASE 6.4   Low Template; Above Threshold

Brothers David and Terence Reed were convicted in 2007 of stabbing their associate Peter Hoe to death in his house in England. It was alleged that two pieces of plastic found at the crime scene were parts of knife handles and that low template DNA analysis of material on them yielded the DNA profiles of both of the brothers.

The contention that LCN DNA evidence might be unreliable was abandoned by the appellant's days before the appeal. The examining laboratory had later repeated the analysis using standard techniques (sufficient amount available) which confirmed the low level results.

The court stated that it was established that the underlying science for low template DNA analysis is sufficiently reliable to produce profiles where the amount analyzed is above the stochastic threshold of between 100 and 200 pg.

The court commented essentially on DNA that was not considered low template/LCN in starting material.

Ambiguity and Stochastic Effects

All methods used to analyze low quantities of DNA suffer from disadvantages of stochastic (random) effects. Stochastic variation is a fundamental physical law of the amplification process when low amounts of DNA are examined. Random sampling effects – called 'stochastic' from the Greek – may occur when a limited number of DNA target molecules exist in a sample. If present in LCN, a DNA molecule will be delivered in variable quantities as a result of sampling variation. This leads to the preferential amplification of alleles.

There are therefore several consequences that cannot be avoided:

- Locus dropout – a whole locus fails to amplify.
- Allele dropout may occur.
- Stutters may increase in size relative to the parent allele.
- Allele dropin results in additional alleles 'contaminating' the sample.

These stochastic effects manifest as a fluctuation of results between replicate analyses. It is possible that amplifying the same extract twice can result in the detection of different alleles at a locus. Since these stochastic effects cannot be avoided when testing small amounts of DNA, two approaches have been proposed: (1) stop testing or interpreting data before the stochastic realm is reached or (2) try to limit the impact by additional testing and following careful interpretation guidelines based on validation studies (consensus and probabilistic models).

The moment that there is acceptance of stochastic effects in a DNA profile there is ambiguity in the interpretation of the DNA profile. Amplification-related stochastic effects create uncertainty about the composition of the crime sample making it difficult to attach a weight of evidence when reference samples are compared to the crime sample.

The 'stochastic threshold' is essentially a risk assessment threshold, where peaks below this level may exhibit stochastic effects. The Scientific Working Group on DNA Analysis and Methods (SWGDAM Guidelines, 2010) describes the stochastic threshold as the peak height at which it is reasonable to assume that the 'sister allele' (say a 16) of a genotype pair (say 15, 16) has not suffered allelic dropout.

There has been discussion about eliminating thresholds such as a 'stochastic threshold' because they represent an artificial cut-off for a phenomenon which is continuous (as described earlier, refer in the definitions). Instead a risk assessment based on peak heights of the resultant DNA profile can be used to determine whether or not an appropriate amount of DNA was present and whether or not stochastic factors impact the result (Balding and Buckleton, 2009; Gill and Buckleton, 2009; Gill et al., 2012; van Oorschot et al., 2010). This is especially the case for mixtures.

DNA evidence from low template profiles was in question in a notorious murder case from Italy (Balding, 2013; Vecchiotti and Zoppis, 2013).

CASE 6.5   Low Template DNA; Interpretation

A British exchange student, Meredith Kercher was murdered in the flat that she shared in the University town of Perugia in Italy in 2007. Rudy Guede pleaded guilty and his conviction was uncontroversial. A flatmate of the deceased, the U.S. student Amanda Knox, and her Italian boyfriend Raffaele Sollecito were also accused of the murder.

The key piece of evidence in the case against Amanda Knox was the DNA obtained from a knife found at Sollecito's flat in the kitchen drawer. The knife allegedly had traces of DNA from Amanda Knox on the handle and of Meredith Kercher on the blade. The DNA alleged to have come from Knox was not disputed (she regularly visited her boyfriend's flat), but the DNA profile alleged to have come from Kercher was low level.

The appeals court experts were asked to repeat, if possible, the genetic analyses carried out during the initial investigation. If a repetition of the analyses was impossible due to insufficient biological material, the experts were asked to examine the technical report drawn up by the scientific police in the course of the first trial.

The quantification analysis performed on the material collected from the blade provided a result far below the value recommended. Since the amount of extracted DNA would not allow a repeat amplification, the appellate court experts decided not to proceed with the genetic analyses on the swabs taken from the knife. The conclusion that exfoliated cells were present on the sample taken from the handle was lacking in scientific basis. Similarly, there was a lack of scientific basis for the inference that there was blood on the knife.

The appeal found that the necessary precautions regarding the testing of low level DNA samples were not followed in the analysis of the DNA from the knife. Furthermore, none of the DNA could be related to blood or any specific biological matter. It was not obvious why the knife was believed to be evidential, and questions were raised about handling and packaging.

After the appeal a further trial found both Amanda Knox and Raffaele Sollecito guilty. Finally, Italy's highest court acquitted both in March 2015 and published their reasons on 7 September 2015 (Supreme Court of Cassation, 2015). The panel of judges found that the state's case had a complete lack of 'biological traces' in connection to the crime. The investigation had been hindered because of investigators under pressure – due to the international spotlight on the case.

Dropout

Investigating ambiguous and low level DNA profiles may not necessarily result in a complete 'match' with the reference DNA profile of a person of interest. Yet, sometimes, the person would be included as a potential match if it could be considered that there was 'dropout' of the non-matching alleles.

Complete locus dropout (that is, no result at all at a locus) is still essentially considered neutral, especially if a repeat amplification does not yield a result. This locus is removed from a statistical calculation. These profiles are partial and still exhibit stochastic effects (incomplete amplification).

Dropout of an allele is considered when the allele that is carried by an individual contributing to a sample (determined from a reference profile from the person) is not reported within a DNA profile obtained from that sample. An alternative explanation is non-concordance or discordance. Dropin occurs when trace amounts of DNA, for example from the crime scene environment or laboratory plastic ware, generate one or more spurious alleles in the profile.

It is rare for dropout or dropin to occur with good-quality samples not subject to degradation or inhibition, but this becomes more likely the lower the amount of DNA or increasing environmental exposure.

Probability of dropout is an estimation of how alleles are expected to fail to amplify, given a low amount of the starting material. The initial theory was developed in 2000 (Gill et al., 2000). The probability of allele dropout is a function of the surviving 'sister' allele height.

It is the 'dropout of an allele' aspect in the interpretation of low template DNA profiles that has proved most problematic. Interpreting data that are not there and assuming there is a flaw in the DNA analysis is controversial. The stochastic effect may also mean that there is dropout of a particular allele in a specific amplification, yet it is amplified in the repeat (not reproducible). It is a more lenient approach to deciding whether a person's DNA can be included.

Figure 6.1 illustrates the concept of 'dropout' of a single allele.

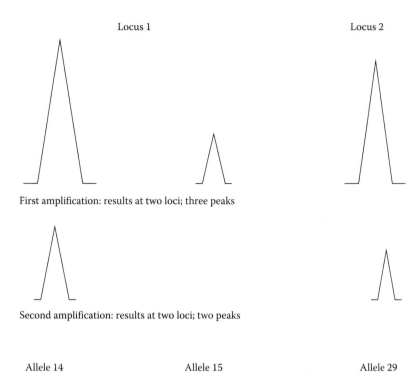

Locus 1   Locus 2

First amplification: results at two loci; three peaks

Second amplification: results at two loci; two peaks

Allele 14   Allele 15   Allele 29

FIGURE 6.1 Dropout of an allele. Diagrammatic representation of peaks observed in a DNA profile; the same sample is amplified twice. Dropout of allele 15 in second amplification. The final profile recorded as [14, -] and [29, -].

An interesting social science study focused on this aspect (Lawless, 2013). The paradigm of the traditional exclusionary aspect of DNA profiling was discussed in contrast to the inclusionary paradigm of low template DNA. Dropout (and dropin) was seen by some to justify decisions about ambiguous data, and a way of merely reinforcing the path an investigation already might have taken.

One of the first uses of probabilistic methods to interpret low level DNA profiles was discussed in the following (Balding and Buckleton, 2009). This article highlighted the problems of the random man not excluded (RMNE) approach to low level mixtures with dropout and discussed two cases, a UK criminal matter and a U.S. criminal matter. The DNA issue in the UK case is summarized as follows (*R v. Garside, Bates*, 2006).

CASE 6.6   Dropout; Low Template; Mixture; Masking; Probabilistic Models

Marilyn Garside was murdered and samples were collected from the crime scene and analyzed for DNA. It was alleged that her estranged husband James Garside had hired Richard Bates to murder his wife. In 2003 James Garside and Richard Bates were convicted in London of the murder. The initial conviction was successfully appealed in 2004, leading to a retrial in 2005 which was followed by an unsuccessful appeal in 2006.

Mixed DNA profiles from the crime scene formed a key part of the evidence. The major component of these crime scene profiles corresponded to the victim and was assumed to be from her (her full profile was available). In addition, up to eight minor component alleles were identified. However, three of Bates' alleles, one at locus D2 and two at locus D18, were not reported in any of the large number of DNA profiles generated in the investigation, from different crime scene samples and different profiling runs under varying laboratory conditions. The proposal that Bates was the origin of the minor component implied that allelic dropout must have occurred at D2 and D18.

The prosecution in effect ignored locus D18 in computing its measure of evidential weight, which was equivalent to a RMNE probability. The authors noted that the widespread policy of ignoring loci showing no minor component alleles is commonly thought to be neutral or conservative, a view sometimes supported by sayings such as 'the absence of evidence is not evidence of absence'. The article showed that in the presence of masking (such as by the victim's alleles), this can be very unfair to defendants.

Talk of 'voids' that may have contained an allele suggests an assumption that dropout has occurred, whereas there may be no 'missing' allele at these loci: the alleles of the true culprit could have been masked by the victim's alleles. In the presence of masking, it cannot be known if any alleles have dropped out, and if so which one(s).

The authors deplored ignoring loci that are discordant with the prosecution case and recommend that dropout and dropin probabilities be assessed.

They also showed the RMNE approach to evidence evaluation had serious flaws in the low template setting and can potentially lead to serious misrepresentation of the evidence.

This report also stated: 'DNA based prosecutions that rely on dropout and do not explicitly state plausible ranges for the dropout probability are, in our view, defective'.

The interpretation of the profile, before the statistical analysis, is important. Determining whether dropout could occur, or whether there could be masking, is required before any statistical analysis.

How a statistical report may list alleles in a table from a low level profile, and how a reader can infer dropout, is described in Table 6.1.

Another example in Table 6.2 describes a mixture of male and female DNA from a female medical swab where often the analysis is 'conditioned' on the female DNA. A single male contributor may be described in a report. Note that there is indication of an extra contribution at only one locus (vWA).

Mixtures

Low template DNA profiles detected in crime profiles tend to be complex mixtures. Statistical analysis of such mixtures is challenging. The interpretation of low level complex DNA mixtures of three or more contributors is fairly common in casework, but is challenging to interpret (Haned et al., 2015).

Table 6.3 describes a mixture of DNA where two suspects may be included as contributors even though their reference DNA profiles do not match (non-concordance).

Mixed samples may be composed of one or more major contributors with high quantities of DNA and with a minor contributor only at trace levels. Alternatively, all contributors' DNA within the mixture may be at trace levels. When there are low

TABLE 6.1 Dropout: Table of Alleles Where Dropout Is Proposed

Locus	D3	vWA	D16	D2	AMEL	D8	D21	D18	D19	THO1	FGA
Crime stain	15,16	14,16,17	10	–	X,Y	11,12,15	28,29,31	12,15	14,15	9.3	–
Victim reference	15,16	14,17	10,11	20,22	X,Y	11,12	29,29	12,15	14,14	9.3,9.3	24,25
Accused reference	15,15	14,16	9,10	19,23	X,Y	12,15	28,31	12,15	14,15	7,9.3	24,26

Notes:
  The names of each locus are along the top row in their usual abbreviated form.
  A partial, mixed DNA profile of at least two contributors is listed.
  There is complete locus dropout at D2 and FGA (no results).
  The victim is proposed to contribute to the crime stain.
  The accused is proposed to contribute to the crime stain.
  Therefore, there must be dropout of the accused alleles – at D16 and THO1.
  Dropout of the alleles from the victim must also be proposed.

TABLE 6.2 Male and Female Mixture—Dropout: Table of Alleles as May Be Shown in a Forensic DNA Report

Locus	D3	vWA	D16	D2	AMEL	D8	D21	D18	D19	THO1	FGA
Medical swab from complainant Seminal fraction	15,17	14,16	10	20	X	12	28	12	14	9.3	24
Epithelial fraction	15,17	16,16	10,10	19, 20	X,X	11,12	28,29	12,12	14,14	7,9.3	24,25
Complainant reference	15,17	16,16	10,10	19,20	X,X	11,12	28,29	12,12	14,14	7,9.3	24,25
Accused reference	15,15	14,16	9,10	20,23	X,Y	12,15	28,31	12,15	14,15	7,9.3	24,26

Notes: A medical swab from the female complainant was obtained; this had very few spermatozoa. It was extracted using a differential lysis technique to obtain any semen material; the DNA profiles in the table correspond to each fraction. The accused is proposed as a contributor to any spermatozoa.

Only one additional allele to the complainant is listed for the seminal fraction (at vWA). Dropout of the accused alleles must be proposed in the 'seminal' fraction if he contributed. The analysis was conditioned on the female contributing DNA due to 'carryover', incomplete separation.

TABLE 6.3 Non-concordance: A Table of Alleles Where Dropout is Proposed for Each Suspect in Order for Their Contribution to the Crime Stain

Locus	D3	vWA	D16	D2	AMEL	D8	D21	D18	D19	THO1	FGA
Crime stain	13,14, 15,16,17	14,16, 17	8,10	–	X,Y	11,12,13, 14,15	29,30.2, 31.2	12,15,16	14,15,16	8,9.3	–
Suspect 1 reference	16,18	14,17	10,11	20,22	X,Y	11,12	29,30	12,15	14,14	9.3,9.3	24,25
Suspect 2 reference	15,16	14,16	9,10	19,23	X,Y	11,15	28,29	12,15	13,14	7,9.3	24,26

Notes:

The crime stain is a partial mixed DNA profile of at least *three* contributors.

There is complete locus dropout at D2 and FGA (no results).

Suspect 1 is proposed to contribute to the crime stain.

Suspect 2 is proposed to contribute to the crime stain.

There is non-concordance of the suspect profiles 1 and 2 with the crime stain profile.

Dropout of the alleles from both suspects must be proposed.

level profiles and there is designated more than one contributor, additional measures need to be taken. The ISFG DNA Commission in 2006 noted that with low level DNA profiles, stochastic effects may limit the usefulness of heterozygote balance and mixture proportion estimates (Gill et al., 2006).

There will be uncertainty in the number of contributors to a low level DNA mixture. Whether such low level mixtures should be interpreted has been discussed for a decade (Lawless, 2013). The uncertainty is high so how can we measure this?

The ISFG DNA commission recommends likelihood ratio methods and provides guidance to interpret complex DNA mixture profiles (Gill et al., 2012):

- Probabilistic methods following the *basic model* described in the guidelines can be used to evaluate the evidential weight of DNA results considering dropout and/or dropin.
- Estimates of dropout and dropin probabilities should be based on validation studies that are representative of the method used.
- The weight of the evidence should be expressed following likelihood ratio principles.
- The use of appropriate software is highly recommended to avoid hand calculation errors.

The introduction of software may introduce problems. A case from the author's files illustrates the problem of interpreting the number of contributors and dropout.

CASE 6.7   Dropout; Low Level Mixture; Number of Contributors

A man was accused of dealing in drugs. A plastic shopping bag from a clothing store was seized. It was believed the accused had carried the drugs in it. A mixed DNA profile of *three* contributors was obtained from the handle areas of the bag.

A statistic was calculated, and it was estimated to be around 500 times more likely that the DNA profile would occur if the accused contributed than if he did not contribute to the DNA. This analysis was performed a few years prior to the trial proceedings – using a 10-marker system. The profile was low level and there was only a partial match of the reference sample of the accused to the crime sample; consequently dropout needed to be proposed.

The statistical weight was calculated using a probabilistic model and computer software. The court then ordered the new typing system of 21 markers be employed on the sample. It was consequently reported that there were four contributors to the mixture. The computer program could not deal with four contributors, and thus no DNA result could be reported.

It was not surprising that there were four contributors to a plastic shopping bag (and possibly more). The initial calculation had been based on an assumption of three contributors that did not explain the later result.

Statistical Approaches

There is ambiguity not only in whether alleles are present but also to which contributor they belong, in low level mixture profiles. The ambiguity complicates not only the estimation of the number of contributors but also the estimation of weight both for and against different propositions.

As yet there is no consensus within the forensic biology community as to the interpretation strategy for these types of DNA profiles (Kelly et al., 2014; Steele and Balding, 2014). The scientific literature is constantly evolving.

Particular approaches for mixtures depend on different models:

- Binary models
- Continuous models

The binary method treats alleles as present or absent.

There is no modification of the binary method that can deal with a non-concordant allele in a comprehensive manner (Buckleton and Triggs, 2006). The binary family of models cannot be used in evaluating low template DNA profiles, where there is the possibility of stochastic effects and dropout. The probability of the evidence according to the prosecution theory cannot be 'one' which is what the binary model assumes (Gill et al., 2012). The only appropriate approach to handling data when there is possibility of allele dropout is to incorporate a probabilistic approach where the probability of allele dropout (and drop in) can be incorporated into the statistic.

Probabilistic genotyping has been introduced to overcome the problems inherent with binary models and in an attempt to interpret low level and/or mixed DNA profiles that are complex in some way.

Some models consider peak heights to inform the model parameters, while quantitative models incorporate peak heights into the statistical likelihood ratio. The description of models as continuous or semi continuous – quantitative or not – itself has been criticised as a false dichotomy (Inman et al., 2015).

A model considered as a 'standard' model for complex DNA profiles has been formally adopted by Euroforgen (Network of Excellence) and can be used by laboratories as a benchmark (Gill and Haned, 2013). Euroforgen is a European Union funded network of excellence that supports open-source initiatives to interpret DNA profiles.

Quantitative models consider peak heights to be continuous random variables and in principle make the 'best use' of available data. However, when amplification stochastic effects such as dropout affect the sample profile (typically low template), these models are less effective because the variability of the signal is exacerbated and the uncertainty in peak heights is difficult to assess. Comparative studies have not properly been undertaken. Consequently, it is not clear how these models behave when applied to low template, and there are little published data (Steele and Balding, 2014).

Because they are based on different assumptions, it is expected that different models will produce different likelihood ratios for a given set of propositions. Little has been published so far that describe the limitations of likelihood ratio models with complex DNA mixtures (Bille et al., 2014; Haned et al., 2015). There has recently been research on the RMNE statistical interpretations for low level DNA profiles which holds promise (Christophe et al., 2015).

Performance Tests

There is a need to validate the particular model used for any given dataset. It is not enough to compare the likelihoods for two competing hypotheses if neither of them can be demonstrated to give a plausible explanation of the data.

If complex DNA profiles, conditioned on multiple individuals, are evaluated, it may be difficult to assess the strength of the evidence based on the likelihood ratio. Models should be considered 'exploratory'. Different propositions, such as different numbers of contributors, may be necessary.

A single likelihood ratio that evaluates a combination of propositions does not give information about the evidential weight per contributor (Dorum et al., 2014). Some caution is required to interpret complex propositions *since the evidential weight per contributor is not provided or indicated by a single likelihood ratio that calculates a combination of propositions.*

One way to address this issue is to further evaluate or qualify the estimated likelihood ratio by a performance test. Based on simulations, this is achieved by non-contributor testing, replacing the reference profile of interest by the profile of a simulated random man (Gill and Haned, 2013; Gill et al., 2015). A suspect centric likelihood ratio requires further testing to determine its 'performance'.

The variation of the likelihood ratios in performance testing provides useful information. Further, research into how juries perceive numerical magnitude is required (Inman et al., 2015). The very large numbers (often billions) produced in likelihood ratios, even with ambiguous DNA profiles, requires exploration.

Open-Source versus Closed-Source Software

The DNA Commission (Gill et al., 2012) advocates open-source software since this solution offers unrestricted peer review and best assurance that methods are fit for purpose.

Availability in an open-source platform ensures transparency of the underlying code and guarantees the possibility of all users to test the robustness of the model (Steele and Balding, 2014).

Some of the software in widespread use in various countries is 'closed source' (Steele and Balding, 2014). Commercial confidentiality creates problems for reviewers – not only in casework.

A culture of reproducibility has been requested for computational research. It should be required for published claims (Peng, 2011; Sandwe et al., 2013).

Freely available open-source software has many benefits, not least the democratic access to both the software package and underlying computer code (see also Inman et al., 2015).

Controversy

Interpretation of low level ambiguous profiles, especially mixtures of three or more people, has been described as an investigatory tool. Whether it can be used as a prosecutory tool is a matter of debate.

A U.S. court decision in 2015 illustrates the diversity of scientific opinion in the interpretation of low template DNA profiles (*People v. Collins, Peaks*, 2015). There was over 2 years of litigation.

Two unrelated violent felony cases were consolidated for the purposes of a Frye hearing. The Forensic Statistical Tool (FST), a computer software application, of the Office of Chief Medical Examiner in New York was used in both cases. It is an in-house statistical tool that computes a likelihood ratio which also models dropout and dropin.

Case 6.8   Low Level Mixtures; FST Statistical Tool; Scientific Consensus

During 2010 in New York, a man was walking along a street when another man on a bicycle started shooting at him. This man jumped off his bicycle and continued shooting at the walker. The assailant then fled. The bicycle was left behind and the investigating police swabbed two areas of the handlebars. It was alleged that Jacquan Collins was the bicyclist.

The swabs were sent to the laboratory. Because the amount of DNA detected was very small, it was analyzed with 'high sensitivity' using 31 cycles. Mixture

DNA profiles were obtained from each swab. Results were reported if two of the three amplifications from the sample agreed (consensus profiles). The FST tool was used to statistically interpret these mixture profiles. One yielded a likelihood ratio of 972,000 where the profile was more probable if the DNA originated from Collins and two unknowns than if it originated from three unknown people. The other mixture was 19.4 times more probable, and not all alleles of Collins were present (dropout proposed). The justice regarded these figures as a reasonable expectation that the evidence would be conclusive on issues of identity at trial.

The defence questioned whether the stochastic effects in the DNA profiles were analyzed through generally accepted methods in the scientific community. They also stated that the FST limits the analysis to single hypotheticals when weighing the statistics.

CASE 6.9   FST Statistical Tool; Scientific Consensus

During July 2010 in New York, victim A was attacked on the sixth floor of a residential building. She was grabbed around the neck and dragged into a stairwell where her attacker touched her breasts and took her purse. When her brother came to her aid, the perpetrator fled, dropping the purse and losing his Yankee cap.

In August 2010 in New York, victim B entered the elevator of a residential building. A stranger got off with her on the seventh floor. He then put her in a choke hold and displayed a box cutter. After taking money from her purse, the attacker ordered her to lift her shirt and bra. When she did so the attacker put his mouth on her breast and then ran from the scene.

The purse and the Yankee cap in the case of victim A were sent for DNA analysis. The cap yielded a mixture DNA profile with a major contributor and a minor contributor from standard DNA tests. The major profile matched the DNA of Andrew Peaks, and there was no issue in the statistical interpretation.

The shirt and the bra from victim B were sent to the laboratory. A DNA mixture was obtained from the bra using standard analysis, and at least three contributors were obtained. These contributors could not be separated into major and minor components. Y-STR profiling was then employed and indicated that a major male component and another male minor component were in the mixture. The defendant's Y-STR profile matched the major profile, indicating that he or a paternal male relative could be the source of the DNA. This particular finding was not in issue.

However, at issue was the result of standard DNA testing of the bra. The interpretation was performed with FST computer software. The defendant's alleles were not found at two of the loci in initial tests. At least one female and two males contributed DNA to the sample. The FST software concluded that it was 19.6 times more likely if the defendant, victim B and an unknown individual contributed than if victim B and two unknowns contributed. The defence stated that the scientific community did not concur with the way that FST assessed the probability of stochastic effects and that the tool does not permit alternative hypotheses.

The judge found that the 'FST' as applied was not generally accepted in the scientific community. Nor was the use of 'high-sensitivity analysis'.

This ruling raised many issues. The statistical interpretation of the DNA results in low level mixtures, and the use of the FST tool for mixtures in general even with standard profiling, was debated for over 2 years. The court found that the particular laboratory validation studies failed to create general acceptance of high-sensitivity analysis. The court also determined that it could not be reasoned that increased stochastic effects in high-sensitivity analysis are of no concern just because there are stochastic effects even with standard analysis.

Another issue was the question of 'black boxes'. The court decided that it was *not* a positive asset that the FST tool remains a black box and that it can only examine the prosecution hypothesis.

How, when or even if low level mixture DNA profiles are interpreted remains a matter of debate.

References

Balding, D. 2013. Evaluation of mixed-source, low-template DNA profiles in forensic science. *Proc. Natl. Acad. Sci. USA* 110(30): 12241–12246.

Balding, D. and Buckleton, J. 2009. Interpreting low template DNA profiles. *Forensic Sci. Int. Genet.* 4: 1–10.

Bille, T.W., Weitz, S.M., Coble, M.D. et al. 2014. Comparison of the performance of different models for the interpretation of low level mixed DNA profiles. *Electrophoresis* 35: 3125–2133.

Buckleton, J. and Triggs, C.M. 2006. Is the 2p rule always conservative? *Forensic Sci. Int.* 159: 206–209.

Butler, J. 2012. *Advanced Topics in Forensic DNA Typing: Methodology.* Elsevier Academic Press: San Diego, CA.

Caddy, B., Taylor, G.R. and Linacre, A.M.T. 2008. A review of the science of low template DNA analysis (Home Office Forensic Regulation Unit). Available online at: https://www.gov.uk/government/uploads/system/uploads/attachment_data/file/117556/Review_of_Low_Template_DNA_1.pdf/, accessed 21 November 2015.

Cale, C.M., Earll, M.L., Latham, K.E. and Bush, G.L. 2015. Could secondary DNA transfer falsely place someone at the scene of a crime? *J. Forensic Sci.* 1–8; first published online 1 September 2015.

Caragine, T., Mikulasovich, R., Tamariz, J. et al. 2009. Validation of testing and interpretation protocols for low template DNA samples using AmpFISTR identifiler. *Croat. Med. J.* 50: 250–267.

Christophe, V.N., Dieter, D. and Filip, V.N. 2015. Effect of multiple allelic dropouts in forensic RMNE calculations. *Forensic Sci. Int.: Gen.* 19: 243–249.

Dorum, G., Bleka, O., Gill, P. et al. 2014. Exact computation of the distribution of likelihood ratios with forensic applications. *Forensic Sci. Int. Genet.* 9: 93–101.

Gill, P., Brenner, C.H., Buckleton, J. et al. 2006. DNA commission of the international society of forensic genetics: Recommendations on the interpretation of mixtures. *Forensic Sci. Int.* 160: 90–101.

Gill, P. and Buckleton, J. 2009. Low copy number typing – Where next? *Forensic Sci. Int. Genet. Suppl.* 2: 553–555.

Gill, P. and Buckleton, J. 2010. A universal strategy to interpret DNA profiles that does not require a definition of low-copy-number. *Forensic Sci. Int. Genet.* 4: 221–227.

Gill, P., Gusmao, L., Haned, H. et al. 2012. DNA commission of the International Society of Forensic Genetics: Recommendations on the evaluation of STR typing results that may include drop out and/ or drop-in using probabilistic methods. *Forensic Sci. Int. Genet.* 6: 679–688.

Gill, P. and Haned, H. 2013. A new methodological framework to interpret complex DNA profiles using likelihood ratios. *Forensic Sci. Int. Genet.* 7: 251–263.

Gill, P., Haned, H. and Bleka, O. 2015. Genotyping and interpretation of STR-DNA: Low-template, mixtures and database matches – Twenty years of research and development. *Forensic Sci. Int. Genet.* 18: 100–117.

Gill, P., Whitaker, J., Flaxman, C. et al. 2000. An investigation of the rigor of interpretation rules for STRs derived from less than 100 pg of DNA. *Forensic Sci. Int.* 112(1): 17–40.

Haned, H., Benschop, C., Gill, P. et al. 2015. Complex DNA mixture analysis in a forensic context: Evaluating the probative value using a likelihood ratio model. *Forensic Sci. Int. Genet.* 16: 17–25.

Hellmann, P. 2011. The Helmann-Zanetti Report. On the acquittal of Amanda Knox and Raffaele Sollecito. Translated into English, 16 December 2011. Available online at: https://hellmannreport.wordpress.com/contents/ reasons-for-the-decision/expert-review-of-exhibits-36-and-165b/, accessed 21 November 2015.

Inman, K.A., Rudin, N., Cheng, K. et al. 2015. Lab Retriever: a software tool for calculating likelihood ratios incorporating a probability of drop-out for forensic DNA profiles. *BMC Bioinformatics.* 16: 298.

Kelly, H., Bright, J., Buckleton, J. et al. 2014. A comparison of statistical models for the analysis of complex DNA profiles. *Sci. Justice* 54(1): 66–70.

Lawless, C. 2013. The low template DNA profiling controversy: Biolegality and boundary work among forensic scientists. *Soc. Stud. Sci.* 43(2): 191–214.

Peng, R.D. 2011. Reproducible research in computational science. *Science* 334: 1226–1227.

People of the State of New York v Jaquan Collins and People of the State of New York v Peaks, Part 26, Indictments 8077/2010 and 7689/2010, Supreme Court, County of Kings, 2 July 2015.

PowerPlex21 System. 2012. Technical manual. Promega Corporation: Fitchburg, WI.

R. v. Broughton. 2010. EWCA Crim 549 36.

R v. Garside, Bates. 2006. EWCA Crim 1395 Royal Courts of Justice, London, U.K.

R v. Hoey. 2007. Judgement, The Crown Court Sitting in Northern Ireland. NICC 49, 20 December 2007.

R v. Reed, Reed and Garmson. 2009. EWCA Crim 2698. Judgment Court of Appeal (Criminal Division), 21 December 2009.

Sandwe, G.K., Nekrutenko, A., Taylor, J. et al. 2013. Ten simple rules for reproducible computational research. *PLoS Comput. Biol.* 9(10): e1003285.

Steele, C. and Balding, D. 2014. Statistical evaluation of forensic DNA profiling evidence. *Annu. Rev. Stat. Appl.* 1: 361–384.

Supreme Court of Cassation Italian Republic. 2015. Marasca-Bruno Motivations Report v 1.2 24 September on the appeals filed by Sollecito and Knox. Fifth penal section.

SWGDAM Guidelines. 2010. SWGDAM interpretation guidelines for autosomal STR typing by forensic DNA testing laboratories. Available online at: https://www.fbi.gov/about-us/lab/biometric-analysis/codis/swgdam-interpretation-guidelines, accessed 21 November 2015.

Taberlet, P., Griffin, S., Goossens, B. et al. 1996. Reliable genotyping of samples with very low DNA quantities using PCR. *Nucleic Acids Res.* 24: 3189–3194.

van Oorschot, R.A., Ballantyne, K. and Mitchell, R. 2010. Forensic trace DNA: A review. *Invest. Genet.* 1: 14.

Vecchiotti, C. and Zoppis, S. 2013. DNA and the law in Italy: The experience of the "Perugia case". *Front. Genet.* 4: 177.

Chapter **7**

Y-STR Profiling and Mitochondrial DNA Typing

Introduction

The genetic markers typed in most forensic biology laboratories are autosomal short tandem repeats (STRs) from the nuclei of cells, Y chromosome STRs and mitochondrial DNA. Y chromosome short tandem repeat (Y-STR) and mitochondrial DNA typing use different techniques to nuclear DNA profiling, and the derivation of the statistical significance is different. The techniques are less discriminatory than nuclear DNA profiling due to the way the different types are inherited – either down the maternal line (mitochondrial) or the paternal line (Y-STR).

Both males and females inherit mitochondria from their mothers. Males (X,Y) in the same paternal line share the same Y-STR profile. Females (X,X) have no Y chromosome at all and therefore cannot be identified by Y-STR profiling.

Mitochondrial DNA is useful in forensic work because it is more abundant and resistant to degradation than autosomal DNA profiling. Y-STR profiling is useful in detecting and separating male material.

The statistical evaluation of nuclear (autosomal) DNA evidence discussed in the previous chapters relies on underlying population genetics. This is also true for lineage markers such as Y-STR and mitochondrial DNA typing.

The statistics for a Y-chromosomal or mitochondrial DNA 'haplotype' are treated mathematically as a single indivisible ('atomic') trait. Thus unlike those traditional DNA methods that examine several traits that are approximately independent of one another, no multiplication of probabilities is possible. The strength of the evidence may depend on the size of the databases.

Y-STR Profiling

Y-STR profiling analyzes the variation on the male (Y) chromosome in nuclear DNA. This technique can be used when autosomal STR (nuclear) DNA typing is unsuccessful on the crime sample and there is male material present in that sample. It is also used when the DNA recovered from an item is both a mixture of male and female DNA. As females do not possess a Y chromosome, this difference is exploited in order to target only the male DNA in a male/female DNA mixture.

Y-STR profiling was used in the following case from Japan, due to the age of the stored medical swabs (Honda et al., 1999).

CASE 7.1   Y-STR; Aged Samples

Two rape/murders and then a rape occurred in Hokkaido in the northern part of Japan, from 1972 to 1973. A man was arrested, confessed to the crimes during the trial, and was sentenced to life imprisonment. A retrial was requested as the suspect later insisted on his innocence. A second trial found that he was guilty and he was sentenced to death. The defence then appealed to the supreme court, but the capital punishment was not overturned. After the judgment of the supreme court, the defence demanded the opportunity of a retrial on the grounds that the judgement based on a confession was unsatisfactory – the original biology evidence of ABO grouping was inconclusive.

DNA was extracted from vaginal swabs collected 25 years previously at autopsy from two victims, one of whom was petrified when found. Differential extraction was not used to avoid further loss of fragile material. Y-STR profiling was performed on the samples and four Y-STR haplotypes were obtained. These were submitted to the court before a reference sample could be obtained from the accused, due to the prosecution requirements. The haplotype results matched the accused haplotype. The high court accepted the results and refused the retrial request in 1998.

Y-STR typing may achieve profiles for male DNA when there are low levels of male DNA and high background levels of female DNA, in mixtures where the female portion is present in overwhelming quantities compared to the male portion, where there are multiple male contributors, or in extended interval post-coital cervicovaginal samples. The following is a brief summary of when Y-STR profiling may be worth considering (Jobling and Gill, 2004):

1. The total number of male cells that are present in a suspected sexual assault may be very small in the case of males who are azoospermic (having no sperm) or oligospermic (having a low sperm count).
2. The total number of male cells may be low due to loss of sample or degradation.
3. Multiple semen donors may need to be identified in a multiple rape case.
4. In criminal paternity or mass disaster victim identification, determination of the haplotype of a missing individual may be conducted by typing a male relative.
5. The inefficient differential extraction procedure for the separation of sperm and non-sperm fractions may be bypassed.

Autosomal STR analysis may fail with some semen samples in which the sperm are present in very low copy number, or are present in a fragile state, such as in extended interval (for example 48 hour) post-coital samples. Differential extraction of these particular samples may yield no profile from the male donor due to a combination of premature lysis of the sperm's cellular constituents into the non-sperm fraction and to sperm loss during the physical manipulations required of the DNA isolation process. Therefore, the use of Y-STRs, which target only the male fraction, eliminate the need for a differential extraction process and lessen the potential to lose the very small amounts of male DNA that may be present (Mayntz-Press et al., 2008).

An interesting case where the Y-STR typing of a large population was used to eliminate suspects, and then autosomal STR profiling used to identify a serial rapist and murderer was performed in Poland in the early 2000s (Dettlaff-Kakol and Pawlowski, 2002).

CASE 7.2 Y-STR Profiling; Mass Screen; Autosomal Profiling

A man committed at least 14 rapes in Poland from 1996 and in the year 2000 murdered a 22-year-old woman. DNA profiles obtained from semen stains gave information that one and the same man had committed all of the rapes. Y-chromosome haplotypes obtained from the semen stains was used in the elimination process of 421 suspects.

One man was found who had an identical DNA profile in all Y-chromosome STR loci analyzed and possessed common alleles in 9 out of 10 autosomal loci, strongly suggesting that the real rapist and the typed man were closely related males. Analysis of reference DNA obtained from the man's brother revealed an identical autosomal STR profile to that identified at the crime scenes.

This Polish case had features in common with familial DNA typing (Chapter 8) and the 'mass screening' approach used in England in the first case where DNA typing was ever used (Case 1.1).

The convention for reporting the significance of matching Y-STR profiles is to state the number of times that this profile occurs in the relevant database (its relative frequency). A forensic scientist might report: The Y-STR profile of the crime sample matches the Y-STR profile of the suspect (at the number of loci examined). Therefore, *we cannot exclude the suspect* as being the donor of the crime sample. In addition, *we cannot exclude all patrilineal related male relatives* and an unknown number of unrelated males as being the donor of the crime sample. The Y-STR profile from Mr. Suspect, which matches that of the crime stain, would be expected to be observed in fewer than 1 in 200 randomly chosen males in the relevant population (database size).

Recommended procedures for the analysis and interpretation of Y-STR profiling have been described (Gusmao et al., 2006; SWGDAM, 2014).

Statistical analyses may be determined for full Y-STR profiles according to defined databases. Partial haplotypes can be used for inclusionary and exclusionary purposes. Indistinguishable mixtures (that is, no major or minor haplotype) may be used for exclusionary purposes. Consensus has not been reached on estimating the occurrence of a combination of haplotypes in a population (mixtures). If reporting an inclusion result from a mixture Y-STR profile the laboratory must perform statistical analysis for support of any inclusion (SWGDAM, 2014).

The exclusionary aspect of DNA profiling (discriminatory) using Y-STR profiling is shown in another case from Japan (Honda, 2013).

CASE 7.3   Y-STR; Exclusion; Aged Samples

A 4-year-old girl was murdered and abandoned on the bank of a river in 1990 (known in Japan as the Ashikaga case). The short-sleeved shirt of the victim had quantities of sperm detected. A suspect Mr. S was identified and later confessed. Both the sperm on the shirt and the reference from Mr. S were said to match in ABO blood grouping (group B) tests and a DNA marker (D1S80). This was the first case where DNA typing was used for a criminal arrest in Japan.

The court accepted the DNA result in 2000 and rejected the defence appeal for a retrial. A DNA retest was granted by the high court in 2008. Nineteen years after the offence, the DNA analysis was considered to be challenging. The shirt was divided between the prosecution and defence experts. The defence selected the piece of shirt with greenish discolouration indicating the presence of semen in which moss and mould could easily grow.

The differential extraction method for semen was not considered suitable. Y-STR profiling was used to exclude the DNA of the victim and improve efficiency of the amplification. The Y-STR results had seven exclusion areas between the shirt sample and Mr. S. The prosecution expert agreed that Mr. S was excluded.

The retrial request was admitted by the court and Mr. S was declared innocent.

These results show that Y-STR profiling is possible from aged semen stains.

Partial and Mixture Y-STR Profiles

The loss of discrimination power for a partial and/or mixture profile is exacerbated in Y-STR profiling. The haplotype is inherited as a unit and when only partially represented, or two or more people may have contributed, any interpretation may be confounded. Sometimes a profile may be used for exclusionary purposes but nothing further can be said due to the inability to determine statistical significance for an inclusion. The investigation of 'cold cases' with the desire to interpret ever smaller quantities of DNA has meant that Y-STR profiling is increasingly used on difficult samples from serious crime. Subsequent issues are being explored at trial – as a case from the United States in July 2015 shows (People v Wright, 2015).

CASE 7.4   Y-STR Profile; Partial; Mixture; Exclusion Versus Inclusion

A man was convicted at trial in 2007 for the murder of a female drug acquaintance and sentenced to a term of twenty-five years to life imprisonment. The defendant stated that he engaged in sexual relations with the victim but did not kill her. The victim was found lying in the driveway of a house, clothed but barefoot, with her hands bound by a shoelace behind her back, and with a shoelace tied around her neck as a ligature.

One DNA prosecution expert testified there were DNA profiles from the hand and neck ligatures that were mixtures of at least two contributors but they were at such a low level there could be no comparisons. 'Transference' was also discussed (DNA could be transferred to the ligatures from other areas). Another expert stated that based on the Y-STR analysis they could not exclude the defendant and the victim's husband as contributors to the hand ligature samples. They could not quantify how many men other than the defendant had the same combination of DNA characteristics.

The Appeals court determined that the defence counsel failed to object when the prosecutor suggested the evidence directly linked the defendant to the murder although it did not and made statements that contradicted the expert testimony about the limitations of Y-STR DNA analysis. As a consequence the defendant was denied a fair trial.

The problems in terminology of 'not excluded' and 'included' and the lack of statistical weight in support of an inclusion is demonstrated in this case.

Mitochondrial DNA Typing

The major advantage of mitochondrial DNA is its multiple copy number per cell. This means that it has a greater probability of survival than nuclear DNA. Forensic applications include analysis of samples that are old, degraded and/or damaged or are low in nuclear DNA such as hair shafts.

Mitochondria are structures within cells (but outside the core or nucleus). They function like 'power plants' providing tools for cells to make energy. The mitochondria are about the size of bacteria and are scattered throughout a cell outside its nucleus. They contain less information than nuclear DNA but because they are smaller, they are also less prone to degradation.

Mitochondrial DNA shares many of the theoretical disadvantages of Y-STR profiling. It is non-recombining so that markers do not segregate independently, thus reducing diversity. It is inherited only through the mother but members of the matrilinear line share the same haplotype.

An appeal in the High Court of Australia concerned the provision of two types of statistics in a murder trial (*Ayturgrul v. The Queen*, 2012).

CASE 7.5   Mitochondrial DNA; Statistics

The deceased and the accused had been in a relationship, but this had ended more than 2 years before the victim was stabbed to death. The prosecution case at trial was circumstantial. A hair was found on the deceased's thumbnail and mitochondrial DNA profiling was performed. It was agreed in the trial that the accused 'could have been' the donor of a hair found on the deceased's thumbnail. The statistics of a mitochondrial DNA profile from the hair with the accused were given as follows:

1. In the general population, 1 in 1600 people would be expected to share the same haplotype (a frequency ratio).
2. The percentage of people who would *not* be expected to have a haplotype matching the hair (an exclusion percentage) is 99.9%.

The accused desired the 'percentage exclusion' figure to be inadmissible. He held that this percentage figure had a 'subliminal' or 'subconscious' impact which invited the jury to approach the case with 'percentages of guilt' and to round up to 100%.

The prosecution expert had used the 'counting method' where the haplotype was observed one time in a database of 4839 individuals of various population groups. A defence expert was of the opinion that 1 in 1000 people in the non-Turkish population would have this haplotype and between 1 and 50 people in the Turkish population would have the haplotype (the appellant was of Turkish descent). These appear to be very different statistics but they are dependent on their derivation. It was discussed in the original trial how the statistics were derived and that mitochondrial DNA profiling was a much less discriminatory technique than nuclear DNA profiling.

The high court dismissed the appeal as it did not consider it was demonstrated that the probative value was outweighed by the danger of unfair prejudice.

Contamination

The bones and teeth are normally the longest-lasting physical evidence of human or animal presence and are also the most widely used samples for ancient DNA studies. However, they are readily contaminated (presumably through handling and washing) and once contaminated in this way are difficult if not impossible to decontaminate. Sparse, damaged endogenous DNA is less likely to be amplified than modern contamination.

A major concern in mitochondrial DNA analysis is contamination of the sample with extraneous DNA (Isenberg, 2005). As an example, a report of dinosaur DNA sequences actually proved to be derived from human DNA contaminating the fossil (Malmstrom, 2005). All samples from 29 dog museum archaeological specimens contained human DNA often at levels exceeding authentic ancient dog DNA.

Even when strict protocols are followed, contaminants are frequently observed. Human DNA has been reported from cave bear samples, 500-year-old pig samples and 109 out of 168 relatively recent fox teeth. Several studies have reported significant numbers of *human* remains contaminated with multiple human sequences (Gilbert et al., 2005).

Mixed mitochondrial DNA profiles in a bone sample indicate that contamination has been introduced into the sample at one stage, that is extraneous DNA not inherent to the bone itself. A single bone or bone fragment belonging to a human should not have a mixed mitochondrial DNA profile indicating contributors from at least two individuals. The following case had mixed mitochondrial DNA profiles in bone samples (from author's case files).

CASE 7.6 Mitochondrial DNA; Bone Sample; Mixture

A man was reported missing. Bone fragments were found at a beach location about a 2 hour drive away. It was alleged that the accused had murdered the victim, burnt his body in a drum and disposed of the bones at the beach.

One bone fragment failed to yield a nuclear DNA profile but gave a mixed mitochondrial DNA profile suggesting the presence of at least two mitochondrial DNA profiles. The prosecution expert stated that the bones were human due to the presence of mitochondrial DNA. Mitochondrial DNA from the bone powder was amplified and sequenced by another laboratory in the United States. Their sequence data also indicated a mixture of two or more mitochondrial DNA profiles, and therefore, the results were inconclusive. Because there was a mixture profile of mitochondrial DNA and a profile could not be assigned to the bone itself, it thus could not be determined whether the bone was human.

If the bones were not originally cleaned sufficiently or a contaminant was introduced at the first examining laboratory, then this will necessarily impact on any subsequent testing by another laboratory. Another analyzing laboratory should be provided with a non-pulverized sample so that their laboratory contamination mitigation measures can be utilized. The mitochondrial DNA evidence was not admitted into trial. The accused was found guilty on other evidence.

Combining Statistics

There is currently no accepted method of combining statistics from autosomal STR profiling with statistics from Y-STR profiling or mitochondrial DNA profiling. There is a different nature of underlying population structure. A combination of the information obtained from lineage genetic markers, such as the Y-chromosome (or mitochondrial DNA), with data resulting from meiotically recombining loci (autosomal STRs) into a single likelihood ratio is generally inconsistent and should be avoided (Amorim, 2008).

More recently a United States group considered that autosomal DNA probabilities may be combined with Y-STR probabilities but work is ongoing (SWGDAM, 2014).

Advances

Advances in technology are used to improve the analysis/interpretation of Y-STR profiling and mitochondrial DNA profiling and overcome some of their limitations. An application of 'cloning' was used in a case from France due to restrictive circumstances. Only a shed hair was available as a reference and there was limited evidence (Hatsch et al., 2007).

CASE 7.7   Cloning; Mitochondrial DNA; Mixture; Incomplete Separation

A woman was raped at knifepoint in France. Semen was found on the medical (vaginal) swabs. Male and female fractions were obtained using a differential extraction technique to separate the sperm from the female material. Autosomal DNA profiling on the male fraction showed an apparent mixture of 1:1 of male and female DNA. A suspect was located a few weeks after this analysis but police only obtained a hair reference sample from him. Nuclear DNA analysis from the hair was unsuccessful (presumably from the hair root), and meanwhile the suspect fled the country. Thus the comparison proceeded with mitochondrial DNA (from the hair to the semen fraction).

Cloning of the mitochondrial DNA sequences was performed. There were matches of cloned sequences between the mixture sperm sample and the victim and suspect reference samples. This finding allowed the prosecution to obtain further reference samples from the suspect from the other country. There was a subsequent nuclear autosomal STR match.

The next chapter discusses some new advances and their application to forensic case work.

References

Amorim, A. 2008. A cautionary note on the evaluation of genetic evidence from uniparentally transmitted markers. *Forensic Sci. Int. Genet.* 2(4): 376–378.

Ayturgrul v. The Queen. 2012. High Court of Australia, HCA 15, 18 April 2012. Respondent's submissions for the High Court S315 filed 21 October.

Butler, J.M. 2012. *Advanced Topics in Forensic DNA Typing: Methodology.* Elsevier Academic Press: San Diego, CA.

Dettlaff-Kakol, A. and Pawlowski, R. 2002. First polish DNA "manhunt" – An application of Y-chromosome STRs. *Int. J. Legal Med.* 116: 289–291.

Gilbert, M.T.P., Rudbeck, L., Willerslev, E. et al. 2005. Biochemical and physical correlates of DNA contamination in archaeological human bones and teeth excavated at Matera, Italy. *J. Archaeol. Sci.* 32: 785–793.

Gusmao, L., Butler, J.M., Carracedo, A. et al. 2006. DNA Commission of the International Society of Forensic Genetics (ISFG): An update of the recommendations on the use of Y-STRs in forensic analysis. *Forensic Sci. Int.* 157: 2–3.

Hatsch, D., Amory, S. and Keyser, C. 2007. A rape case solved by mitochondrial mixture DNA analysis. *J. Forensic Sci.* 52(4): 891–894.

Honda, K. 2013. The Ashikaga case of Japan – Y-STR testing used as the exculpatory evidence to free a convicted felon after 17.5 years in prison. *Forensic Sci. Int. Genet.* 7: e1–e2.

Honda, K., Roewer, L. and de Knijff, P. 1999. DNA typing from 25-year-old vaginal swabs using Y-chromosomal STR polymorphisms in a retrial request case. *J. Forensic Sci.* 44: 868–872.

Isenberg, A. 2005. Forensic mitochondrial DNA analysis. In *Forensic Science Handbook*, Vol. II, Saferstein, R. (ed.). Pearson Prentice Hall: Upper Saddle River, NJ.

Jobling, M.A. and Gill, P. 2004. Encoded evidence: DNA in forensic analysis. *Nat. Rev. Genet.* 5: 742–751.

Malmstrom, H., Storra, J., Holmgund, G. et al. 2005. Extensive human DNA contamination in extracts from ancient dog bones and teeth. *Mol. Biol. Evol.* 22: 2040–2047.

Mayntz-Press, K.A., Sims, L.M., Hall, A. et al. 2008. Y-STR profiling in extended interval ($\geq$3 days) postcoital cervicovaginal samples. *J. Forensic Sci.* 53(2): 342–348.

People v Wright. 2015. NY Slip Op 05621, Decided 1 July. Court of Appeals Rivera J.

Scientific Working Group on DNA Analysis Methods (SWGDAM), Interpretation guidelines for Y-chromosome STR typing. January 2014. Available online at: https://www.thermofisher.com/content/dam/LifeTech/Documents/PDFs/SWGDAM_YSTR_Guidelines_APPROVED_01092014_v_02112014_FINAL.pdf, accessed 21 November 2015.

Introduction

Advances in technology have meant that the DNA molecule can be analyzed in different ways to that described in the previous chapters. New DNA techniques have been used for medical purposes. The latest technologies have been used in conjunction with mitochondrial DNA and Y-STR profiling to identify bones in 'ancient' DNA.

These new technologies have been thought useful for analyzing DNA left at crime scenes. The techniques described in this chapter are used as a 'last resort' when routine DNA profiling is unsuccessful. They are used in an investigative way, much like DNA profiling was used in the first forensic DNA case in England (Case 1.1). They attempt to narrow down the potentially enormous pool of suspects in a criminal matter when no suspect has been initially identified.

These techniques may be pushing the boundaries of what is legally acceptable in DNA profiling. The ethics of the particular test may be in question. Different jurisdictions may deal with a particular test in different ways. The following DNA tests are just some of these new technologies that have been used, or proposed, for criminal investigations.

Familial DNA Searching

A DNA profile (from the traditional method) may be found at a crime scene for which there is no suspect. A routine search of a DNA database is often used to find a matching DNA profile. However, this may not yield any 'match'. It is now possible to conduct a search on the database to identify potential relatives of the donor of the crime stain. This search is based on the number of shared genetic characteristics (the alleles) and the rarity of those shared alleles in human populations. This is called familial searching and has been implemented in the United Kingdom and elsewhere (Gill et al., 2015).

DNA databases are traditionally designed to rely on a full or partial DNA match (all alleles available in the sample) with the crime scene sample. Familial DNA searching utilizes partial matches (*not* partial profiles), and further DNA interpretation is required for the particular search method.

This extension of the purpose of DNA databases has proved ethically controversial. If the donor of the crime stain is not recorded on the database, then no match will result. However, close relatives such as a brother or a father will have many alleles in common. Rather than search for a complete match, a search that relies on more than half of the alleles matching will yield a list of potential suspects that may be quite large.

The United Kingdom pioneered the use of familial DNA searching. One of the first criminal cases where familial searching was used was the Valentine's Day murder of Lynette White in 1988 in South Wales (Exhibit A, 2004).

CASE 8.1   Cold Case; Exhibit Re-Examination; Familial DNA Searching

A woman was murdered in her bedroom in her flat above a betting shop in Cardiff. She had more than 50 stab wounds, an almost severed head, and there were indications of male blood at the scene. Five local men were arrested, one being her 'pimp'. The first trial did not finish due to the death of the judge. The second trial was in 1990 and three of the five accused were convicted of murder. However, these convictions were quashed on appeal in 1992.

A cold case review was launched in the year 2000, and all the exhibits were sent to a different forensic laboratory. A partial male DNA profile was obtained from a blood spot on a cellophane cigarette packet. It was postulated that the offender may have cut himself during a frenzied attack.

The scientists went back to the original flat and found that it had been repainted. They examined the skirting board below the original splashes of blood seen in the crime scene photographs. Three weeks of scraping back the paint revealed traces of the original bloodstains, and a full DNA profile was obtained from the blood that matched the 'cellophane man'. Eventually, the 'cellophane man's' blood was found in 10 places in the flat, on and around the deceased's body and the exit route. The DNA profile was placed on the national DNA database but no match was found. However, there was an uncommon allele in this DNA profile. This DNA profile was then searched on the South Wales database for a family-type match. One profile stood out which was a 14-year-old boy born after the offence. His uncle Jeffrey Gafoor gave a DNA sample to police and it matched the cellophane man. Jeffrey Gafoor pleaded guilty and was convicted in 2003.

Unlike a search for a direct match, a familial search will allow for matching subsets of alleles at any given genetic marker as a basis for comparison. A familial search relies on mathematical modelling specific to the DNA database being utilized. This modelling determines whether an observed similarity between two DNA profiles is more likely the result of kinship or mere chance (Myers et al., 2010). It is more time-consuming and labour intensive than traditional statistical approaches.

Not all jurisdictions have supported the technique, and there is concern over technical pitfalls and the value of familial DNA testing when balancing privacy issues (Butler, 2012).

The following case of the Grim Sleeper was notorious in the United States. The Grim Sleeper case was the first time an active familial search was used to solve a homicide case in that country (Butler, 2012; Steinhauer, 2010).

CASE 8.2   Cold Case Series; Familial DNA; Y-STR Match

The murders of 10 young women in a city from the United States were linked through firearms analysis and DNA. The murders were from 1985 to 2007, and the perpetrator was called the 'Grim Sleeper' as there was a 13-year gap in detected crimes.

A familial search of DNA database profiles in 2010 yielded one likely relative to the crime scene profiles, a DNA profile added to the database in 2009 after a felony weapons charge. Profiles from the Grim Sleeper crime scenes shared one allele at all 15 loci with this felon. This meant that it was possible the felon was a relative of the Grim Sleeper; they also shared the same Y-STR profile. Police had a suspect, the father of the felon, and followed him. They had an undercover police officer who acted as his waiter in a pizza restaurant, and the waiter collected his discarded utensils and pizza leftovers so that a comparison DNA profile could be compared. There was a full autosomal STR DNA match with the crime scene profiles. The accused pleaded not guilty.

A large volume of exhibits dating back 30 years has caused a lengthy pretrial discovery, and the case is continuing as of July 2015.

Twins

The DNA from related individuals has more in common than a random person. Because siblings inherit DNA equally from each parent, some DNA fragments at each locus could be the same. Twins are a special case. Fraternal twins come from two eggs from the mother that are fertilized by the same sperm, so their DNA may be different. Identical twins – also known as monozygotic twins – have been considered genetically identical. The fertilized egg splits in two.

There is a probability of identical twins in about 3 in 1000 births (Weber-Lehmann et al., 2014). Thus it is not surprising that crime cases with identical twins can occur and sometimes receive a high level of attention. The concept of the 'evil twin' is a historical fascination. Identical twins also present legal problems. Most often neither twin can be prosecuted because it is not possible to tell which one was responsible. A famous jewellery heist in Germany presented a legal conundrum (Himmelreich, 2009).

CASE 8.3   Trace DNA; Identical Twins; Legal Conundrum

During January 2009 in Berlin, Germany, $6.8 million of jewellery was audaciously snatched from a luxurious department store. The store had a sophisticated security system. Surveillance cameras depicted three masked and gloved people sliding down ropes from the store's skylights. A DNA profile was found on a latex glove left at the scene and run through the national DNA database to find a match with two people – identical twins. They were charged with the heist, but before the trial they were released. The court determined that at least one of the brothers was responsible – but they could not determine which one.

The problem of identical twins may also be encountered in cold cases. The following case is from the author's files.

CASE 8.4   Cold Case; Database Match; Identical Twins

A 'cold' case of sexual assault on a woman two decades ago was reinvestigated. A DNA profile was obtained from the semen from a stored medical swab from the woman, which also matched a DNA profile from a stored semen stain from her underpants.

There was a match of the evidentiary DNA profiles with that from a suspect and he was charged. It was then alleged that he had an identical twin. This twin had allegedly been in the examining forensic laboratory on a guided tour for the public at approximately the same time the exhibits were examined. The judge ordered analysis of the DNA profile of the accused's twin. The case is ongoing.

A new test developed by Eurofins, a company in Germany, has found that there may be rare genetic mutations in single-nucleotide polymorphisms (SNPs, pronounced 'snips'). This test evaluates different sequences in the human genome from that usually evaluated in casework, which are short tandem repeats (STRs). Only one case has been studied and published, that of identical twins with a child, in 2014 (Weber-Lehmann et al., 2014). The company now accepts casework. The test takes many weeks and is relatively expensive compared to 'routine' DNA profiling. Reference samples from each supposed twin need to be supplied.

Domestic Animal Hair

Many homes in many countries have domestic companion pets such as cats and dogs. These animals readily shed hair on the clothing and the environment of humans. It is thus likely that this type of evidence can occur at crime scenes, either on the clothing of the victim/perpetrator or at the scene itself. Today the reality of DNA profiling of animal hairs has increased the potential of this type of evidence. However, in the author's general casework experience, this type of evidence is either ignored or used as a last resort. Testing of non-human DNA samples is not routinely performed in forensic laboratories.

The first criminal case using animal hair DNA (autosomal STR typing) was that of "Snowball', a white cat that belonged to the parents of a murder suspect (Menotti-Raymond et al., 1997).

CASE 8.5   Cat Hair DNA; Autosomal STR

The body of a 32-year-old woman Shirley Duguay was found in a shallow grave in a wooded area on an island in Canada in 1994, some 8 months after she disappeared. A man's jacket had been found 8 km from her house 3 weeks after she had gone missing. The leather jacket was covered in blood stains matching the DNA of the deceased but also had numerous white cat hairs on the lining. The estranged boyfriend Douglas Beamish was living with his parents and they had a white cat called 'Snowball'.

The cat hair on the jacket had sufficient DNA from the roots to perform nuclear STR analysis. The DNA profile obtained matched that of Snowball. A statistic was obtained from a database compiled from other cats on the island. The case set a legal precedent allowing animal DNA to be admitted as evidence in criminal trials. Douglas Beamish was convicted of murder and sentenced to 15 years in prison.

Cats have 18 pairs of autosomal STRs and the sex chromosomes X and Y. The commercially available 'Meoplex' kit contains 11 STR markers (Butler et al., 2002).

Sufficient DNA for STR typing is generally only obtainable from the root of a hair and not the shaft. Mitochondrial DNA from the hair shaft of humans has been well investigated (Chapter 7). A study from 2011 found that mitochondrial DNA could be obtained from cat hairs without a root (Tarditi et al., 2011). Mitochondrial control region databases for cats have been developed.

The first time that cat hair DNA was used in the United Kingdom was in a murder case and required compilation of a mitochondrial cat DNA database by the University of Leicester (Press Release, 2013).

CASE 8.6   Cat Hair; Mitochondrial DNA

The dismembered torso of David Guy was found on a beach in England wrapped in a curtain. Eight cat hairs were found on the curtain and linked to a cat called 'Tinker' belonging to a suspect, a neighbour of the deceased.

Mitochondrial DNA from the hairs matched that of Tinker, and this type was not found in a database of 493 randomly sampled United States cats. The investigating police wanted to know the statistics for the UK cats. A UK cat mitochondrial DNA database was not in existence, so the University of Leicester compiled 1 from 152 cats around the country. Only three samples in the database had a mitochondrial DNA type that matched that of Tinker. This evidence was used at trial as part of the case. The accused was convicted and sentenced to life imprisonment.

It has been discovered that fewer cats are needed for these types of mitochondrial databases in order to perform statistics, than humans or dogs (Grahn et al., 2015). However, so far the statistics are still limited and do not provide the discriminatory power of human DNA profiling.

Forensic DNA Phenotyping

DNA profiling in criminal cases has traditionally studied the variations in the non-coding regions of a person's DNA. 'Coding' regions of the DNA molecule are now being investigated. Predicting externally visible characteristics such as hair colour and eye colour is known as forensic DNA phenotyping (abbreviated as FDP). This technique uses SNPs rather than STRs.

Most work has focused on pigmentation genes, and it has been found that one gene has a large influence on eye and hair colour. The HIrisPlex test predicts both hair and eye colour and can type as little as 63 pg (picograms) of starting DNA (Walsh et al., 2013). This test has limitations such as inability to predict age-related hair changes.

DNA phenotyping is used for ancient remains to inform our understanding of the past. The oldest forensic case to date has been the recent identification of bones that used mitochondrial DNA, Y-STR profiling and FDP (King et al., 2014; Press Release, 2014).

CASE 8.7   Phenotyping;
Mitochondrial DNA; Y-STR

A skeleton was excavated in 2012 from the last known resting place of the medieval English King Richard III. This king was a controversial figure, suspected of murdering his two nephews, and Shakespeare modelled him as a villain. He was the last of the Plantagenet kings and the last English king to die in battle, at the young age of 32. The battle was in 1485 and called 'The Battle of Bosworth Field'.

The king's physical appearance was historically recorded as having one shoulder higher than the other. The excavated skeleton appeared to have scoliosis which accorded with the uneven shoulders. There were no contemporaneous portraits in existence as all of them post-dated his death by at least 25 years. However, a portrait termed the 'arched-frame portrait' was used for comparison. DNA-predicted hair and eye colour using the HIrisPlex kit was blond hair and blue eyes. This was believed to be consistent with the king's appearance in the portrait as blond hair in youth could darken with age (the king appeared to have dark hair in the portrait).

Reference saliva samples were obtained from living relatives of the king. Mitochondrial DNA analysis from the remains had sequences that matched two living relatives. Y-chromosome haplotypes did not match which could be attributed to a false paternity event occurring in any of the intervening generations.

The work concluded there was overwhelming support that the remains were King Richard III thus closing an over 500-year-old missing person case.

Very small amounts are required for phenotyping kits as they use the smaller fragment SNPs. Contamination is an issue at these small levels. There are legal and ethical problems in the use of this technique because it is from coding regions of a human.

FDP has been considered useful for investigative purposes because a sample left at a crime scene is 'abandoned material'.

Once a suspect is obtained, then traditional DNA typing should be used in comparison of samples. Most countries only allow the use of non-coding DNA in criminal investigations and prosecutions.

Mini-STRs

A minifiler STR kit uses 'mini' STR markers that are reduced in size compared to the autosomal STR kits traditionally used. The reduced size enables better recovery of information from degraded DNA samples by improving amplification efficiency (Butler, 2012).

Microbial Forensics

Microbial forensics studies variations in bacteria and viruses and is yet another emerging field (Budowle, 2011). Microbial evidence can be obtained from real terrorist events or hoaxes. There are practical difficulties in determining the type and strain (hazardous material) and then potential origin.

During 2001 in the United States, the bacteria anthrax was in anonymous letters sent in the mail to government offices and media outlets. This resulted in 22 anthrax cases and 5 deaths. A breakthrough was announced in 2008. A government scientist at an institute for infectious diseases was suspected of sending the letters, but he committed suicide before any charges (Butler, 2012).

Botany

DNA is now being investigated in cases where distinctive plant material, including pollen from a scene may be linked to a suspect or victim (Butler, 2012). This type of associative evidence can be used in a way similar to domestic animal hair.

References

Budowle, B., Ed. 2011. *Microbial Forensics*, 2nd edn. Elsevier Academic Press: San Diego, CA.

Butler, J.M. 2012. *Advanced Topics in Forensic DNA Typing: Methodology*. Elsevier Academic Press: San Diego, CA.

Butler, J.M., David, V.A. and Menotti-Raymond, M. 2002. The MeoPlex: A new DNA test using tetranucleotide STR markers for the domestic cat. *Profiles in DNA* 5(2): 7–10.

Exhibit A. 2004. *News from Forensic Alliance*, Issue 1. Forensic Alliance: Abingdon, U.K.

Gill, P., Haned, H. and Bleka, O. 2015. Genotyping and interpretation of STR-DNA: Low-template, mixtures and database matches – Twenty years of research and development. *Forensic Sci. Int. Genet.* 18: 100–117.

Grahn, R.A., Alhaddhad, H., Alves, P.C. et al. 2015. Feline mitochondrial DNA sampling for forensic analysis: When enough is enough. *Forensic Sci. Int. Genet.* 16: 52–57.

Himmelreich, C. 2009. Despite DNA evidence, Twins charged in heist go free. *Times Online*, 27 March 2009. Available at: http://content.time.com/time/world/article/0,8599,1888126,00.html, accessed 25 November 2015.

King, T.E., Fortes, G.G., Balaresque, P. et al. 2014. Identification of the remains of King Richard III. *Nat. Commun.* 5(5631): 1–8. Available online at: http://www.nature.com/ncomms/2014/141202/ncomms6631/full/ncomms6631.html, accessed 25 November 2015.

Menotti-Raymond, M., David, V.A. and O'Brien, S.J. 1997. Pet cat hair implicates murder suspect. *Nature* 386: 774.

Myers, S.P., Timken, M.L., Piucci, G.A. et al. 2010. Searching for first-degree familial relationships in California's offender DNA Database: Validation of a likelihood ratio-based approach. *Forensic Sci. Int. Genet.* 5(5): 493–500.

Press Release. 2013. Leicester forensic experts create UK's first cat DNA database. University of Leicester: Leicester, U.K., 14 August 2013.

Press Release. 2014. King Richard III: DNA and genealogical study confirms identity of remains found in Leicester and uncovers new truths about his appearance and Plantagenet lineage. University of Leicester: Leicester, U.K., 2 December 2014.

Steinhauer, J. 2010. 'Grim Sleeper' arrest fans debate on DNA use. *The New York Times*, 8 July 2010. Available online at: http://www.nytimes.com/2010/07/09/us/09sleeper.html?_r=0, accessed 25 November 2015.

Tarditi, C.A., Grahn, R.A., Evans, J. et al. 2011. Mitochondrial DNA sequencing of cat hair: An informative forensic tool. *J. Forensic Sci.* 56(Suppl. 1): S36–S46.

Walsh, S., Liu, F., Wollstein, A. et al. 2013. The HIrisPlex system for simultaneous prediction of hair and eye colour from DNA. *Forensic Sci. Int. Genet.* 7(1): 98–115.

Weber-Lehmann, J., Schilling, E., Gradl, G. et al. 2014. Finding the needle in the haystack: Differentiating "identical" twins in paternity testing and forensic testing by ultra deep next generation testing. *Forensic Sci. Int. Genet.* 9: 42–46.

Chapter **9**

Quality

Introduction

Forensic science evidence should be demonstrated to be reliable and valid – essentially, demonstrate the quality. The quality of a forensic examination is a matter of consideration for every case. Quality failures may be encountered in forensic DNA profiling evidence. Quality control systems in laboratories aim to *mitigate* and monitor such failures.

The technique of DNA profiling is performed and interpreted by human beings – although at many steps in the analytical process humans are being replaced by robots (e.g. the extraction stage, Chapter 4). Errors in quality are errors in interpretation. Highly publicized cases of quality failures illustrate problems in a particular case and in a particular way as shown in the cases discussed. Furthermore, instances of quality failure can be encountered in 'routine' casework, also described later.

A well-known failure of quality control occurred in Germany a few years ago (Daniel and van Oorschot, 2011; Himmelreich, 2009).

CASE 9.1   Quality Failure;
Contamination; Background DNA

A mystery female offender was known as 'The Phantom of Heilbronn', the woman without a face. She was believed to be Germany's most dangerous woman. She was not only a brutal killer (suspected of at least six murders) but also a common thief. Forty unsolved crimes over 15 years were linked by DNA to the phantom, including the murder of a policewoman in Heilbronn. The phantom's DNA was found at a car dealership burglary and a school break and enter, but in both cases her convicted 'accomplices' denied her existence.

The real phantom was discovered when officials, trying to establish the identity of a burned corpse from the fingerprints from an asylum application form, found the form to contain the phantom's DNA. As this was thought impossible, they repeated the analysis to find that the DNA was not there. It was ultimately discovered that the cotton swabs used to collect DNA material were contaminated. Although these swabs were sterilized for medical use, this process may not destroy DNA, and some of the swabs contained enough cellular DNA for DNA profiles. The origin of the DNA was eventually traced back to an innocent woman working in a cotton swab factory.

This case highlighted the importance of testing for 'background DNA' from items used in the examination process. Recommendations relating to manufacturers of laboratory products have since been made to ensure laboratory reagents, and materials are DNA-free in addition to being sterile (Gill et al., 2010).

An interesting study which explored this problem was on unused gloves (Daniel and van Oorschot, 2011). DNA was observed on gloves from closed boxes and thought to have originated from the manufacturing process. Unless specified, it should not be assumed that laboratory gloves (packaged and/or sterile) are DNA-free.

Contamination

It is known that viruses can readily transmit a disease to humans and other species – the common 'cold' is an example. Precautions can be taken to prevent colds (such as removal from human contact), but a person may not know when or how the cold virus was transmitted to them. Recent outbreaks of the Ebola virus in Africa have shown that medical personnel can be infected if personal protection equipment is not secured.

Contamination in a case regarding DNA profiling results involves the concept of DNA transfer (see Chapter 3).

There is no specific 'test' for contamination. Audit trails may follow the path of the exhibit from collection to final analysis and indicate areas in which contamination may be a possibility. Other evidence may indicate that it was physically impossible for the accused to have committed the crime (such as being in prison at the time or overseas).

A young woman was falsely implicated in a murder in Australia over a decade ago (Johnson, 2006).

CASE 9.2   Contamination;
Case to Case Transfer

The body of a very young child was found in a lake some 6 months after he went missing. He was dressed in a bib and trousers. A trial jury acquitted the mother's de facto, who was also the babysitter at the time of the murder.

A DNA profile was obtained in 2003, years after the trial, from the child's clothing. This DNA profile matched the DNA profile of a young woman who was a complainant in a rape case. Her reference DNA profile was obtained to compare to the condom in the rape case. Police could find no connection between the woman and the dead child.

The laboratory stated there was an 'adventitious match' although there was an extremely small chance of matching the DNA from the child's clothing with a random person. The coronial inquest in 2006 discovered that the child's clothing was examined within days of the condom from the rape case by the same forensic scientist. None of the child's own DNA was found on his clothing, and the clothes had been submerged in muddy water for 6 months, which raised the question of why any DNA was found at all.

The coroner found that contamination had occurred in the laboratory although the exact pathway could not be determined. The coroner also found that the explanation of the adventitious match with another person with the same DNA profile meant that a person of interest was still at large, which he did not accept.

Contamination can be sporadic and not global, that is not on every exhibit. The moment of contamination may not be known.

Contamination depends on the availability and opportunity of DNA transfer. Some ways to detect this include an assessment of the scientific interpretation (part of which includes an independent review) and exploration of continuity (see further sections).

A government inquiry into a false conviction in Australia reiterated the problems of contamination.

> It is almost incredible that, in consequence of a minute particle, so small that it was invisible to the naked eye, being released into the environment…a chain of events could be started that culminated in the conviction of an individual for a crime that had never been committed by him or anyone else, created immense personal distress for many people and exposed a number of deficiencies in our criminal justice system. But that, I believe, is what happened.
>
> **Vincent, 2010**

An appeals court in an Italian murder trial commented on the possible contamination of exhibits collected at crime scenes (Gill, 2014; Hellmann, 2011). An argument had been put that it was not enough for the defence to say that the DNA result was from contamination – the burden was on those claiming contamination to prove its origin. However, the appeals court held that the 'burden' was in showing the result was obtained using a procedure which guaranteed the integrity of the item, from the moment of collection to the moment of analysis. Once there was no proof that these precautions were taken, then it is not necessary to also prove the specific source of the contamination.

Possible avenues of contamination should be considered. Using collecting/detection devices on multiple exhibits and at multiple scenes can introduce minor or gross contamination. Fingerprint brushes, for example, are able to transfer amounts of DNA between exhibits that could generate profiles and may retain biological evidence for a considerable period of time (van Oorschot et al., 2005). DNA deposited on one item can thus be transferred to another.

Controls

Running negative controls throughout the entire process may be part of a laboratory quality process. A reagent blank control is that consisting of all reagents used in a particular process but contains no sample. These controls do not offer protection against contamination before the process.

Elimination DNA databases of scientific staff and investigators should be maintained. If contamination is detected, the contaminant DNA profile can then be searched against the elimination database.

Laboratories should be tested regularly for the presence of contaminating DNA. The increased sensitivity of DNA profiling means that enhanced anti-contamination measures are required (Ballantyne et al., 2013). This type of quality system is called 'environmental monitoring' described in Chapter 3.

Substrate controls have traditionally been examined to determine if the substrate (such as fabric in clothing) on which the stain was deposited contained any material that might interfere with the interpretation of the stain. In the age of DNA profiling, this type of 'testing in parallel' may not be performed.

An early DNA case used substrate controls from a crime scene (*People v. Simpson*, 1995; Thompson, 1996). The prosecution contended that cross-contamination of blood drops at the scene of the deaths was ruled out because substrate controls (taken from unstained areas adjacent to the blood drops) were negative – that is they contained no detectable DNA. However, it appeared that the substrate controls were not run in parallel thus leaving open the possibility that the substrate controls were not exposed when any contamination occurred.

Continuity

Continuity and audit trails may assist in querying the potential for error at each step. An audit trail of a sample should have a unique identifier that enables the sample to be followed at each stage of the analysis so that questions such as which scientist handled the sample on a particular date and location can be readily answered.

The importance of continuity is always stressed in forensic examinations. A check of the continuity records may reveal quality errors such as contamination. Continuity checks may reveal quality failures that may not be expected. The following bizarre case from England shows a consequence of transcription error and contamination (Davies, 2012; Satter, 2013).

CASE 9.3 Transcription Error; Continuity; Contamination

A Welsh mathematician and code breaker, Gareth Williams was attached to MI6 (a UK intelligence organization) at the time of his death in 2010. His decomposing naked body was found in the bathtub of his flat in London over a week after he was last seen. The body was padlocked inside a sports bag. He had no injuries and no illicit or poisonous substances in his body. The keys to the padlock were underneath his naked body (inside the bag), and the police originally determined he could not have locked himself inside.

The inquest in April 2012 heard that there was a transcription error in the DNA profile when a forensic scientist asked for a DNA check. This led police to believe there was foreign DNA on the bag and body. It was only discovered in early 2012 that the DNA was a partial profile that may have belonged to a police scientist investigating the crime scene.

> The inquest found that an unknown party had locked Gareth Williams inside his sports bag. A police re-investigation in 2013 concluded that the death was probably accidental.

The importance of continuity was described in the trial of a man accused of a bombing in Northern Ireland (*R v. Hoey*, 2007; Rennison, 2012). Justice Weir stated that the court

> …must be satisfied by the prosecution witnesses and supporting documents that all dealings with each relevant exhibit have been satisfactorily accounted for from the moment of its seizure until the moment when any evidential sample relied upon by the prosecution is taken from it and that by a method and in conditions that are shown to have been reliable. This means that each person who has dealt with the item in the intervening period must be ascertainable and be able to demonstrate by reference to some proper system of bagging, labelling, and recording that the item has been preserved at every stage free from the suspicion of interference or contamination. For this purpose they must be able to demonstrate how and when and under what conditions and with what object and by what means and in whose presence he or she examined the item….

Transparency

There should be clear and transparent documentation in case files and reports. The standard is that another scientist in the discipline should be able to review the reports and come to the same conclusion as the reporting scientist. The scientific reasoning of the reporting scientist should be readily discoverable and a reviewer should not be forced to wade through procedures and protocols of the laboratory.

If a scientist expresses an opinion, then this must be qualified by experimental evidence. If an opinion is expressed that appears to have no supporting data (in terms of peer review or data analysis) so that it cannot be tested objectively, then it has no scientific basis.

The notes of the forensic scientist should be 'contemporary', written at the time of the examination or as close as possible to it.

The investigation of 'cold cases' from years prior (when DNA profiling was not used) may reveal documents that are brief and do little to describe the actual examination, where it was performed and on what date. The lack of contemporaneous note taking may introduce doubt, and past examiners may be required to produce statements years after an event. These statements may only be capable of saying it was 'normal practice' to perform an examination a certain way. Exhibits may be lost or destroyed and only sections or swabs taken still remain in the older cases.

A trial in the United Kingdom was concerned with a lack of contemporaneous note taking (*R v. Smith*, 2011; Rennison, 2012).

> …No competent forensic scientist in other areas of forensic science these days would conduct an examination without keeping detailed notes of his examination and the reasons for his conclusions…As neither the original examiner nor those who confirmed his examination made any notes of their reasons and did not identify the points of comparison contemporaneously on a chart, it was not possible to see whether their reasoning was the same.…

The lack of contemporaneous note taking in a case, and where analysts rely on memory, may result in a particular type of cognitive bias called 'reconstructive effects'. Gaps are filled in with what analysts believe should have happened and thus they may be influenced by protocol requirements when recalling events some time later from memory (Tully, 2015).

Interpretation

DNA results in a report should be accompanied by assumptions and limitations. It may not be obvious that another expert in the case has considered the limitations. The following is from the author's files.

CASE 9.4   Equivocal Result; Support of Another Opinion

Two young men were travelling in a motor vehicle at a high speed on a country road. Both men were ejected from the vehicle which was found on its roof. No other vehicles were involved and there were no witnesses. One man was found dead at the scene with multiple injuries. The other man was charged with culpable driving causing death as it was believed he was the driver.

The prosecution relied partly on DNA evidence. There was DNA on swabs from the passenger side and DNA from one swab from a blood stain on the passenger seat belt of the car. The DNA profiles matched the DNA profile of the deceased. No DNA was found matching the accused. The results were listed in a table with the statistical weighting in favour of one hypothesis over another (and not the likelihood ratio, possibly transposing the conditional). Assumptions or limitations were not described.

The DNA results were equivocal, providing no support for the location of either man in the car at the time of the accident. Another expert, but not in DNA profiling, used the DNA results to support an opinion that the accused was the driver.

The judge directed that the experts involved gather together before trial and determine issues that were in agreement and issues in disagreement. Shortly before trial, the prosecution discontinued proceedings.

Ambiguous results that are subject to alternative interpretations can be encountered in DNA profiling. Mixture DNA profiles and low amounts of DNA are obvious examples. Transfer mechanisms of trace DNA are also problematic as Chapter 3 describes.

How to interpret ambiguous DNA profiles is still a matter of debate in the literature. Performance testing of likelihood ratios, or non-contributor testing, has been described (Chapter 5; Gill and Haned, 2013).

'Examiner bias' or 'cognitive bias' are terms used to describe subjective judgements especially with regard to ambiguous results. This type of thinking was described by epidemiologists in relation to 'cancer clusters' in cities (Gawande, 1999). It was defined as 'the tendency to assign unwarranted significance to random data by viewing *post hoc* in an unduly narrow context.' It is to reason from the conclusion to the supporting premises.

A case with fluctuating DNA statistics was from the author's files.

CASE 9.5   Selective Sampling; Subjective Statistics

A man was charged with blackmail, and it was alleged he sent threatening letters to the two complainants. He denied sending the letters, which were in envelopes stamped and sealed with sticky tape. The son was also allegedly involved in the offence but was not charged as he gave evidence against his father.

No reference sample was obtained from the son, only the accused. There was only one pertinent DNA result in the case out of a total of 16 DNA results. Trace DNA was obtained from a piece of sticky tape and seal area of an envelope and letter. The first forensic report had the DNA as a mixed profile from at least two contributors. It was considered 120 million times more likely if the accused and one other contributed DNA than if two unknown people contributed. A second report was issued by another scientist as a result of a method review, and this time the DNA was considered to be a single source with a partial DNA profile. It was considered 90 million times more likely if the accused was the origin of the DNA than if an unknown person was the origin.

The profile was low template but not described as such. The nature of the method review was also not described. Only one reference sample was analyzed.

Understanding the cognitive nature of subjective decision making means that steps can be made to increase the value of those decisions – such as counter measures that minimize contextual influences and biases (Dror, 2013).

A series of articles on cognitive bias in science was recently published by the journal 'Nature' (Nature editorial, 2015). A pertinent comment was that analyses should be labelled as 'exploratory' or 'confirmatory'. This is relevant to DNA forensic science in the courtroom context. Although alternative propositions may be considered in the statistical evaluation of likelihood ratios, for example, these propositions may still be 'exploratory'. Different likelihood ratios may be produced from different sets of propositions for one suspect DNA contributor(s), especially in complex mixed and low level DNA profiles (see Chapter 6). The statistic produced is thus 'exploratory' and not confirmatory, and should be described as such in any report and/or testimony.

Guidance to mitigate cognitive bias in the practice of forensic science was also recently published by the United Kingdom forensic regulator (Tully, 2015). The guidelines explain the terminology used in cognitive bias and areas where it may occur, such as interpreting ambiguous results in any forensic discipline. An interesting case example from 2013, involving the authors of the guidelines, is given involving cognitive bias in the interpretation of complex mixed DNA profiles. Further, the requirement of replication (duplication or multiple analyses) in low level/complex DNA profiles is emphasised.

Error Rate

How often mistakes are made is a basic requirement in science and known as the 'error rate'. The following has often been asked by some forensic science commentators – why is it necessary to have match probability data on DNA profiles (the rarity of a DNA profile) but not the probability there is a wrong result? The high numbers generated in DNA profiling of match probabilities appear to overwhelm all argument. But the probability of a wrong result is a different question.

There are many steps in the processing of a DNA sample, and at each step, there can be a potential for error. These steps include identification of the biological stain/material on the item, extraction of the DNA, quantification of the DNA, amplification and separation of the components and finally interpretation, including statistical interpretation. Many cases are usually processed at the one time.

The probability of error tends to completely dominate the value of the likelihood ratio in DNA statistics – possibly rendering the rarity of the corresponding characteristics virtually ineffective (Taroni et al., 2013). There is a clear argument that current knowledge does not allow the probability of error to be anywhere as small as the vanishingly small conditional probabilities quoted in laboratory statements, even from complex low level DNA mixtures.

Even though forensic DNA analysis is often seen as the 'gold standard' of forensic science, error rates in casework have not been published at a detailed level (Kloostermann et al., 2014). There is still discussion and confusion about the definition and relevance of error rates, the estimation of them and the communication to the legal justice system. There has been criticism that there is a lack of transparency concerning mistakes.

The only known laboratory error rates are those defined where there is an outside audit of the laboratory or when there has been a corrective action documented by the laboratory. Corrective actions are those instances where samples have been known to produce a false match. Quality assurance procedures should incorporate corrective actions. These records are often confidential.

One particular quality failure was reported at the Netherlands Forensic Institute (Kloostermann et al., 2014). An offender had been identified as 'The Avenger of Zuuk'.

CASE 9.6   DNA Contamination; Laboratory Staff

The DNA profile of an unknown woman in a series of arson and anonymous threats was identified from one of the postal items. More than 50 women volunteered to provide their DNA in a mass screening in the Dutch rural community of Zuuk.

It was later found that the supposedly incriminating DNA profile was the result of laboratory contamination.

> The DNA profile matched that of an NFI technician. The mass screened reference samples from the town of Zuuk were destroyed.

The only detailed study to date regarding DNA error rates is that from the Netherlands Forensic Institute (Kloostermann et al., 2014). They concluded that their frequency of quality failures was comparable to studies from clinical laboratories and genetic testing centres (quality issue notifications at about 0.5% of cases). The most common causes of failures related to the laboratory process were contamination and human error. Most human errors could be corrected, whereas gross contamination in crime samples often resulted in irreversible consequences. A very limited number of cases had crucial errors detected after the report was issued, sometimes with severe consequences. Many of these errors were made in the post-analytical phase.

Reliability and Validity

It is necessary that a DNA result is reliable. A lay person may ask the question – can we trust the results? Are they reliable?

Reliability in a science experiment is measured by accuracy and reproducibility. A result may be reproducible yet not be correct (or 'accurate'). A quote attributed to Einstein is '...insanity is doing the same experiment over and over again and expecting different results'.

Replication (repeating) of a DNA result can reduce concerns about error, especially when there is a possibility of a false positive (such as contamination) due to poor scientific practices.

Reproducibility

Recent concern was expressed regarding some biomedical studies and this was described in a journal editorial (Mcnutt, 2014):

> Science advances on a foundation of trusted discoveries. Reproducing an experiment is one important approach that scientists use to gain confidence in their conclusions. Recently,

the scientific community was shaken by reports that a troubling proportion of peer-reviewed preclinical studies are not reproducible....

A consensus on reporting principles to improve quality control in biomedical research and encourage public trust in science was published in the November 2014 journal of *Nature* (Editor, 2014). It was recommended that journals should strongly encourage, as appropriate, that all materials used in the experiment be shared with those who wish to replicate the experiment.

DNA results should rely on a similar foundation.

Validation and Peer Review

Validation of a particular DNA method is the process of providing evidence that it is fit for purpose. External validation of the method is often that done in developmental work. Internal validation of forensic DNA methods is an evaluation in the particular reporting forensic laboratory.

Validation studies in forensic science should be publicly available and usually published (Edmond et al., 2014). However, with 'closed-source' statistical programs (expert systems), there may be commercial aspects that prevent this. There has been recent discussion regarding 'open-source' and 'closed-source' programs in the statistical analysis of DNA profiles (Gill et al., 2015).

Disclosure, either public or institutional, is essential to controlling conflict of interest, and some universities and scientific journals prohibit certain forms of commercial contractual arrangements by their members or authors.

The National Science and Technology Council's Subcommittee on Forensic Science in 2015 noted that

- It was unclear in some cases which literature citations were crucial to support the foundation of a particular forensic science discipline
- Some of the cited literature had not undergone a rigorous peer review process

There has been recognition that more research is required in the forensic science disciplines. This is so even in DNA analyses considered to be the 'gold standard'. The interpretation of DNA is much more than a statistical result and more research is required in the transfer, persistence and context of DNA found at a crime scene.

A core element of many of the new statistical models in DNA interpretation is the computer code. The 'Nature Journal' encourages as much code sharing as possible for reproducible research (Nature editorial, 2014).

References

Ballantyne, K., Poy, A.L. and van Oorschot, R.A. 2013. Environmental DNA monitoring: Beware of the transition to more sensitive methodologies. *Aust. J. Forensic Sci.* 45(3): 323–340.

Daniel, R. and van Oorschot, R.A. 2011. An investigation of the presence of DNA on unused laboratory gloves. *Forensic Sci. Int. Genet. Suppl.* 3: e45–e46.

Davies, C. 2012. Gareth Williams inquest hears of mystery DNA at crime scene. *The Guardian*, 24 April 2012. Available at: http://www.theguardian.com/uk/2012/apr/24/gareth-williams-mi6-dna-death, accessed 25 November 2015.

Dror, I. 2013. Editorial – The ambition to be scientific: Human expert performance and objectivity. *Sci. Justice* 53: 81–82.

Editorial. 2014. Journals unite for reproducibility – consensus on reporting principles aims to improve quality control in biomedical research and encourage public trust in science. *Nature*, 5 November. Available at http://www.nature.com/news/journals-unite-for-reproducibility-1.16259, accessed 25 November 2015.

Editorial. Nature. 2015. Let's think about cognitive bias. *Nature* 526, 163, 8 October. Available at: http://www.nature.com/news/let-s-think-about-cognitive-bias-1.18520, accessed 4 December 2015.

Edmond, G., Martire, K. and Kemp, R. 2014. How to cross-examine forensic scientists: A guide for lawyers. *Aust. Bar Rev.* 39: 174–197. Available at: http://netk.net.au/Forensic/UNSW1.pdf, accessed 25 November 2015.

Gawande, A. 1999. The cancer-cluster myth. *The New Yorker*, 8 February 1999, pp. 34–37.

Gill, P. 2014. *Misleading DNA Evidence: Reasons for Miscarriage of Justice*. Academic Press: London, U.K.

Gill, P. and Haned, H. 2013. A new methodological framework to interpret complex DNA profiles using likelihood ratios. *Forensic Sci. Int. Genet.* 7: 251–263.

Gill, P., Haned, H. and Bleka, O. 2015. Genotyping and interpretation of STR-DNA: Low-template, mixtures and database matches – Twenty years of research and development. *Forensic Sci. Int. Genet.* 18: 100–117.

Gill, P., Rowlands, D., Tully, G.G. et al. 2010. Manufacturer contamination of disposable plastic-ware and other reagents – An agreed position statement by ENFSI, SWGDAM and BSAG. *Forensic Sci. Int. Genet.* 4: 269–270.

Hellmann, P. 2011. The Helmann-Zanetti Report. On the acquittal of Amanda Knox and Raffaele Sollecito, translated into English. Available at: http://hellmannreport.wordpress.com. Accessed 16 December 2011.

Himmelreich, C. 2009. Germany's phantom serial killer: A DNA blunder. *Time Magazine*, 27 March. Available at http://content.time.com/time/world/article/0,8599,1888126,00.html, accessed 25 November 2015.

Johnson, G. 2006. State Coroner, Inquest into the death of Jaidyn Raymond Leskie. Coroner's Case No. 007/98. Melbourne, Victoria, Australia.

Kloostermann, A., Szerps, M. and Quak, A. 2014 DNA error rates in forensic DNA analysis: Definition, numbers, impact and communication. *Forensic Sci. Int. Genet.* 13: 77–85.

McNutt, M. 2014. Editorial – Reproducibility. *Science* 17: 3413. Available at: https://www.sciencemag.org/content/343/6168/229, accessed 4 December 2015.

National Commission on Forensic Science. 2015. Scientific literature in support of forensic science and practice. National Institute of Standards and Technology. Available at: http://www.justice.gov/sites/default/files/ncfs/pages/attachments/2015/01/21/scientificliteraturereviewsdocument-finaljan2015.pdf, accessed 25 November 2015.

Nature Editorial. 2014. Code Share – Papers in Nature journals should make computer code accessible where possible, 29 October. Available at: http://www.nature.com/news/code-share-1.16232, accessed 25 November 2015.

People v. Simpson. 1995. California Supreme Court of Los Angeles County. Case BA097211.

R v. Hoey. 2007. The Crown Court sitting in Northern Ireland NICC 49, 20 December.

R v. Smith. 2011. EWCA Crim 1296.

Rennison, A. 2012. Information. Legal obligations, Issue 1. Forensic Science Regulator FSR-I-400. Available at: https://www.gov.uk/government/uploads/system/uploads/attachment_data/file/118893/legal-obligations-issue-1.pdf, accessed 25 November 2015.

Satter, R. 2013. Gareth Williams British spy likely died in bag by accident. *Huffington Post*, 11 March 2013. Available at: http:// http://www.huffingtonpost.com/2013/11/13/gareth-williams-accident-died-in-bag_n_4266397.html?ir=Australia, accessed 4 December 2015.

Taroni, F., Biedermann, A. Vuille, J. and Morling, N. 2013. Whose DNA is this? How relevant a question? (a note for forensic scientists). *Forensic Sci. Int.: Gen.* 7: 467–470.

Thompson, W.C. 1996. DNA evidence in the O.J. Simpson trial. *Univ. Colorado Law Rev.* 67(Fall): 827–857.

Tully, G. 2015. Cognitive bias effects relevant to forensic science examinations. FSR-G-217 Issue 1 Forensic Science Regulator 30 October. Available at: https://www.gov.uk/government/publications/cognitive-bias-effects-relevant-to-forensic-science-examinations, accessed 4 December 2015.

van Oorschot, R.A.H., Treadwell, S. and Beaurepaire, J. 2005. Beware of the possibility of fingerprinting techniques transferring DNA. *J. Forensic Sci.* 50(6): 1–6.

Vincent, H.F. 2010. Inquiry into the circumstances that led to the conviction of Mr Farah Abdulkadir Jama. Victorian Government Printer: Melbourne, Victoria, Australia.

Glossary

Allele	Alternative at a site on the DNA molecule; one alternative is inherited from each parent; variation at a given locus on a chromosome; number of short tandem repeats at a locus in a chromosome.
Amelogenin	Marker used to characterize the sex of an individual.
Amplification	Process by which the number of copies of specific DNA sequences are increased via a sequential copying process.
Analytical threshold	Minimum height requirement at and above which detected peaks can be reliably distinguished from background noise on an electropherogram.

Artefact	Result occurring in the DNA profile (electropherogram) from process rather than intrinsic to the DNA tested; see stutter and pull-up.
Autosome	Chromosome not involved in sex determination; humans have 22 pairs of autosomes.
Chromosome	Discrete unit of the genetic material carrying genes and arranged into structures which can be visualized during cell division.
CODIS	Combined DNA Index System database for DNA profiles used in the United States.
Combined probability of exclusion (CPE)	1 – CPI.
Combined probability of inclusion (CPI)	Approach to statistical analysis in mixtures; produced by multiplying the probabilities of inclusion from each locus; probability of including a person in a mixture profile; binary model; problem using with complex mixtures and dropout.
Conditional	An interpretation category that incorporates assumption(s) as to the number of contributors.
Confirmatory test	Test used to confirm the presence of a particular biological material such as blood or semen.
Contamination	Extraneous DNA from a source not associated with the crime stain – for example plastic ware contaminated at manufacturing source.
Crime scene sample	Sample taken from a crime scene or body by either a crime scene investigator or medical personnel.
Degradation	Breakdown of the DNA strand through age, environment or chemical insult resulting in a greater loss of the longer fragments.

Deoxyribonucleic acid (DNA)	Chemical compound found in all nucleated cells of the body; codes for the characteristics in humans.
Differential extraction or lysis	Method to separate sperm and epithelial cells in a mixture by preferentially lysing; sperm DNA recovered by centrifugation.
Dropin	Contamination from a source not associated with the crime stain and manifested as one or two alleles.
Dropout	Low level of DNA insufficiently amplified to give a detectable signal.
Electropherogram	Instrumental output showing DNA profile in the form of peaks on a graph.
Electrophoresis	A method of separating molecules based on size and charge, used to separate DNA fragments of varying length by the application of an electric current.
Exclusion	Exclusion from a stain: a decision (by the expert) that a particular reference DNA profile does not represent a contributor to the stain.
Exclusion probability	Probability that a randomly selected DNA profile would be excluded.
Familial searching	Process which allows potential relatives of offenders to be identified on the DNA database when the offender profile is not on the database.
Frequency	Rate at which an event occurs. For example, sample frequency of an allele is the number of occurrences of the allele in a population sample, divided by the sample size: population frequency of a DNA profile is the (unknown) number of times that the profile occurs in the population, divided by the population size.

Gene	Site on the DNA molecule. A sequence of the code inherited for which there is a functional product; sequence of DNA base pairs.
Genome	Entire genetic material of an organism contained in a full set of chromosomes.
Genotype	Characterization of alleles at a particular site; the designation of two alleles at a locus is a genotype.
Guidelines	A set of general principles used to provide directions and parameters for decision making.
Haplotype	Collective genotype of a number of linked loci on a chromosome that are inherited together; in mitochondrial DNA, the sequence of the control regions of mitochondrial DNA that pass from a mother to her offspring unchanged.
Heterozygote	The two alleles possessed by an individual at a particular site are different.
Homozygote	The two alleles possessed by an individual at a particular site are the same.
Intelligence-led screens	Conducted during major crime investigations; investigates a DNA sample from a crime scene with a number of people who may have been associated; a view to elimination.
Likelihood	Conditional probability of an event, where the event is considered as an outcome corresponding to one of several conditions or hypotheses.
Likelihood ratio	The ratio of two probabilities of the same event under different hypotheses; the numerator typically contains the prosecutor's hypothesis and the denominator the defence hypothesis; often expressed as the ratio between the

	likelihood that a given profile came from a particular individual and the likelihood that it came from a random unrelated person.
Locus	Name given to the area of DNA that is analyzed when generating a DNA profile. Several locus are called 'loci'.
Low level or low template or low copy number DNA analysis	Term used when very small amounts of DNA are analyzed, typically producing peaks below the 'stochastic' level.
Major contributor(s)	An individual(s) who can account for the predominance of the DNA in a mixed profile.
Masking	Occurs in a DNA mixture where there is overlap of the same allele originating from different contributors.
Minor contributor(s)	An individual(s) who can account for the lesser portion of the DNA in a mixed profile.
Mitochondrial DNA	DNA obtained from the mitochondria of the cell.
Mitochondrion	A subcellular unit within the cell which provides the cell with energy (plural is mitochondria).
Mixture	A DNA typing result originating from two or more individuals.
Mixture ratio	The relative ratio of the DNA contributions of multiple individuals to a mixed DNA typing result, using quantitative peak height information; may be expressed as a percentage.
Molecule	A chemical substance consisting of atoms bound together in a specific structure.
Multiplexing	A method of amplifying multiple sites on the DNA molecule in one reaction vessel.

Nuclear DNA (nDNA)	The DNA found in the nucleus of a cell; nuclear DNA testing; includes both autosomal STR DNA typing and Y-STR DNA typing.
Nucleus (plural nuclei)	Structure in a cell that contains most of the DNA.
Partial profiles	May result when the sample is deficient in either quality or quantity so that a full profile is not produced.
Phenotyping (also known as forensic DNA phenotyping [FDP])	Predicting externally visible characteristics such as hair colour and eye colour; uses SNPs rather than STRs.
Polymerase chain reaction (PCR)	Technical name for the DNA amplification process where one or more regions of the DNA are copied using a DNA polymerase enzyme so that enough DNA is generated for analysis.
Polymorphism	Occurrence of more than one form or type.
Presumptive tests	A screening test used to indicate the possible presence of the named body fluid.
Primer	Synthesized sequences of DNA that are complementary to a specific segment of the DNA on either side of the area of interest and are used in the PCR process; each primer is fluorescently labelled so that the copied STR allele can be visually detected and its length measured.
Probability	Rate of occurrence of an event in a repeatable experiment; expected frequency; a number between zero and one that reflects in a reasonable way belief that the event is true.

Profile	The STR alleles detected in numerical format; one or more genotypes used for DNA comparison.
Propositions	The hypothesis of the defence or prosecution arguments that are used to formulate the likelihood ratio.
Pull-up	An artefact resulting from the fluorescent detection process.
Random man not excluded (RMNE)	The probability that a random person (unrelated individual) would not be excluded as a contributor.
Random match probability (RMP)	The probability of randomly selecting an unrelated individual from the population that has the same DNA profile as that of the questioned sample; mRMP, modified random match probability; the major and minor components in a mixture can be separated, and the random match probability is calculated as if the component was from a single source sample.
Relative fluorescent units (RFU)	Unit of measurement of peak heights on an electropherogram involving detection of fluorescence intensity.
Resolvable DNA mixture	Mixture of two or more individuals' DNA detected from an item of evidence in which the ratios of major and minor contributors can be deduced due to the proportion of one versus the other.
Sex chromosomes	Chromosomes involved in the determination of the sex of an individual. Females possess two X chromosomes and males possess one X and one Y chromosome.
Short tandem repeat (STR)	Type of repeat unit known to vary at locus on the DNA molecule; used to generate DNA profiles in nuclear DNA typing.

SNPs	Single-nucleotide polymorphisms on the DNA molecule; smaller than short tandem repeats (STRs); low discrimination.
Stochastic	Random; variation in detection of alleles on repeat sampling with small amounts of DNA.
Stochastic effect	Imbalance in the amplification of two alleles competing during PCR, where one allele is preferentially amplified over the other.
Stochastic threshold	Minimum quantity of DNA to produce a 'reliable' or 'optimum' profile; can assume that allelic dropout of a sister allele has not occurred at a particular locus above this threshold; determined in particular laboratory studies.
Stutter	Allelic artefact caused by 'slippage': one repeat unit less than the allele that causes the stutter; 'overstutter' can occur which is one repeat longer than its associated allele.
Touch DNA	DNA that is left behind, typically from skin (epithelial) cells; when a person touches or otherwise comes into contact with an item or other person; now superseded by the term trace DNA as often not known that the DNA was transferred by touching.
Trace DNA	DNA that cannot be associated with a biological deposit such as blood or semen; not necessarily a small amount.
Wearer DNA	DNA that is associated to habitual wearer of garment.
Y-STR profiling	DNA typing in which STRs are analyzed on the Y, or male, chromosome.

Bibliography

Gill, P., Brenner, C.H., Buckleton, J.S. et al. 2006. DNA commission of the International Society of Forensic Genetics: Recommendations on the interpretation of mixtures. *Forensic Sci. Int.* 160: 90–101.

Puch-Solis, R., Roberts, P., Pope, S. and Aitken, C. 2012. Practitioner guide 2 – Assessing the probative value of DNA evidence. Royal Statistical Society: London, U.K.

SWGDAM STR Interpretation Guidelines. 2010. Available at http://www.swgdam.org/#!publications/c1mix, accessed 22 November 2015.

Index